Greening the Workplace

Pascal Paillé

Greening the Workplace

Theories, Methods, and Research

Pascal Paillé
NEOMA Business School—Campus Rouen
Rouen, France

ISBN 978-3-030-58387-3   ISBN 978-3-030-58388-0   (eBook)
https://doi.org/10.1007/978-3-030-58388-0

Cover illustration: © John Rawsterne/patternhead.com

This Palgrave Pivot imprint is published by the registered company Springer Nature
Switzerland AG
The registered company address is: Gewerbestrasse 11, 6330 Cham, Switzerland

CONTENTS

LIST OF FIGURES

CHAPTER 1

Introduction

Abstract This chapter provides an introduction to the greening of work-places. The core of this book is developed through three key ideas. The first is that the looming environmental crisis challenges the viability of the general choices that underlie the development of our society. Second, the perspective adopted in this book implies approaching greening from the point of view of individuals in nonmanagerial positions. Third greening is examined through one characteristic often attributed to organizations is their power to act—a power that is itself diluted within a vague and elusive whole.

Keywords Overview · Aims · Employee level

> Capitalist production only develops [...] by simultaneously undermining the original sources of all wealth—the soil and the worker.
> K. Marx, *Capital*, Volume 1

This book examines the greening of workplaces. The term "greening of workplaces" will be used to mean the various measures implemented by and within organizations with the aim of making workplaces more environmentally friendly, less energy-intensive, and more consistent with the ethical standards imposed by the need to take environmental issues into consideration.

© The Author(s) 2020   1
P. Paillé, *Greening the Workplace*,
https://doi.org/10.1007/978-3-030-58388-0_1

The idea for this book was borne out of a personal realization, which is that there is an inherent contradiction in the very nature of our current understanding of the role of human agency in environmental degradation. Sources of GHG emissions are either natural or man-made. Natural emission sources include volcanoes, forest fires, and natural processes (source: ALCEN Corporate Foundation). Most natural sources (around 43%) are related to exchange processes between the oceans and the atmosphere, while emissions generated by nonhuman living beings and soil decomposition account for the remainder in roughly equal measure (28.5%). 87% of CO_2 emissions from human activities are generated by fossil fuel combustion (coal, oil, and natural gas). Finally, another interesting fact is that the management (collection and treatment) of waste generated globally by human activities is estimated to account for 5% of GHG emissions (source: Futura, 1 November 2018).

In the case of man-made sources, GHG emissions are generated by businesses and households, the two main categories of operators. Stern (2000) noted that "much of the environmental impact of human activity results from the actions of organizations, not individuals, and from organizational decisions about production and service provision, not consumption" (p. 524). Similarly, Davis and Challenger (2009) reported that "according to recent government statistics, the impact of the non-domestic sector (e.g. services, public sector and industry) is significantly higher than that of residential users" (p. 112). In other words, the contradiction is this: the knowledge developed in this area over the last thirty years shows that efforts so far have largely focused on households rather than organizations, despite the overwhelming evidence that businesses have a significantly greater impact on the environment than households. Put simply, we know a lot about agents that have a minor impact and comparatively less about those that do the most harm to the environment.

Three key ideas lie at the core of this book.

The first is that the looming environmental crisis challenges the viability of the general choices that underlie the development of our society. More generally, the crisis sheds doubt on the ability and willingness of major greenhouse gas emitters to overhaul the human and industrial organization on which our model of economic development is based (Bell, Greene, Fisher, & Baum, 2001). However, the recent environmental literature provides evidence of numerous initiatives geared toward taking environmental considerations into account at all levels within organizations. Both the professional and the generalist literature include examples of publications aimed at setting out the simple procedures, habits, and routines that we can all perform at work in order to reduce the carbon footprint on a day-to-day basis. The value of such publications lies in the fact that they help to draw attention to the simplicity of environmental actions at an individual level. However, they also neglect to consider the influence of a whole range of contextual factors that have the potential to promote personal inertia. Paradoxically, a high degree of routinization in daily tasks is needed for simple eco-friendly habits to become embedded, raising the question of the importance accorded to the environment in work processes.

Second, the perspective adopted in this book implies approaching greening from the point of view of individuals in nonmanagerial positions. The main reason for examining the question from this perspective is that the individual level remains the least studied level of investigation. The point is to direct the focus of attention toward individuals who are not responsible for managing a team or who have not been delegated any authority—in other words, toward individuals acting as subordinates in roles and positions overseen and managed by other people acting as their superiors. Put differently, the aim is to understand how and why a subordinate behaves (or does not behave) in a particular way by taking environmental considerations and characteristics into account in their day-to-day work. The interesting point is that, though they may lack the powers and attributes of a manager, subordinates can demonstrate leadership in some circumstances. Someone in a managerial position may lack leadership, while someone who is not a manager may demonstrate leadership skills. What is true in general is also true at an environmental level. It seems to me that this distinction is crucially important.

The third key idea is linked to the second. One characteristic often attributed to organizations is their power to act—a power that is itself diluted within a vague and elusive whole. Immersed in their subjectivity, employees rely on people with whom they interact on a regular basis. The human resource management literature reminds us that the way in which employees behave at work is closely linked to the managerial skills of their immediate supervisors. Depending on their agenda, the latter may or may not act as facilitators in this regard. This is an important point. Immediate supervisors have a significant ability to shape and influence not only work behaviors, but also environmental behaviors. The implications of this point are critically important and will be a recurring theme throughout the book.

Finally, this book is neither an essay nor a handbook. It is not an essay since it does not purport to defend or uphold a particular thesis, and it is not a handbook since no general overview or summary is provided. Rather, my intention is to discuss a set of related issues by examining the greening of workplaces from a range of different perspectives. The more modest aim of this book is to share some ideas and to set out some key questions and thoughts, often in the form of carefully argued positions, but sometimes also proffered as modest propositions designed to arouse curiosity and to encourage debate on environmental issues in organizational contexts. Each issue will be addressed as a standalone chapter. Although they are clearly linked by the same overarching theme, and while references to previous issues discussed will be included at various points throughout the book, the different chapters can be read independently. The book discusses the main theories and related fields surrounding studies on environmental behaviors in workplace settings, the different forms of environmental engagement, their main drivers and obstacles, and the notion of environmental performance. A deliberate decision was made not to offer a literature review on the determinants of environmental behaviors. The reason for this is that a number of excellent overviews and summaries are already available in the literature, making any such attempt here superfluous and unnecessary. Interested readers are referred to the various handbooks published in recent years (Robertson & Barling, 2015; Wells, Gregory-Smith, & Manika, 2018). The book also proposes an original model developed with the aim of understanding how obstacles to the adoption of environmental behaviors operate in practice—specifically, a new integrative model of (non)environmental behaviors based on individual decision-making. The book concludes by examining the links between organizational practices, individual behaviors, and environmental performance.

References

Bell, P. A., Greene, T. C., Fisher, J. D., & Baum, A. (2001). *Environmental psychology*, (5th ed.). London and Belmont, CA: Thomson Wadsworth Belmont.

Davis, M. C., & Challenger, R. (2009). Climate change—Warming to the task- Matthew C. Davis and Rose Challenger argue that it's time for psychology to lead the way in greening behaviour. *Psychologist, 22*(2), 112–114.

Robertson, J. L., & Barling, J. (Eds.). (2015). *The psychology of green organizations*. USA: Oxford University Press.
Stern, P. C. (2000). Psychology and the science of human-environment interactions. *American Psychologist, 55*(5), 523–530.
Wells, V. K., Gregory-Smith, D., & Manika, D. (Eds.). (2018). *Research handbook on employee pro-environmental behaviour*. UK: Edward Elgar Publishing.

CHAPTER 2

Key Issues, Evidence and Human Activities

Abstract This chapter provides some key issues. The subject is approached from the perspective of employee subjectivity rather than the organization as a whole, which, however coherent it may be as both an entity and a research perspective, often tends to be viewed as devoid of personality. The aim is to provide points of reference with a view to illustrating how members of an organization exert pressures on the natural environment through their professional activities.

Keywords Evidence · Organizational activities · Human activities

2.1 THE ENVIRONMENTAL CRISIS: KEY ISSUES AND EVIDENCE

2.1.1 Prolegomena

As a sign of the times, it has become increasingly common to come across the subject of ecology and the environment as a theme in works of popular culture. A good example is the movie *The Day the Earth Stood Still*, in which Klaatu, an alien visitor from a distant world, comes to Earth to warn humans that they are threatening the future of mankind. The nature of the threats posed by mankind has changed over the last fifty years. In the original 1951 version, director Robert Wise emphasized

P. Paillé, *Greening the Workplace*,
https://doi.org/10.1007/978-3-030-58388-0_2

7

the nuclear risk and the irreversible damage caused by nuclear warfare. In the 2008 remake, Scott Derrickson chose the environmental crisis as the backdrop for a retelling of the story. As the saying goes, reality is sometimes stranger than fiction.

2.1.2   Mounting Evidence

Current evidence suggests that human activities are the cause of ongoing large-scale changes, leading some to speak of the emergence of an entirely new geological epoch known as the Anthropocene. The term was coined by Crutzen and Stoermer in a May 2000 publication in which the authors posited that the Holocene came to an end around the 1750s with the emergence of a new epoch coinciding with industrial development. According to Crutzen and Stoermer (2000), the presence and concentration of greenhouse gases (carbon, methane and nitrous oxide), or GHG, are one of the main characteristics of the Anthropocene. The World Meteorological Organization found recently that the concentration of GHG in the atmosphere has increased significantly since the pre-industrial era, and there is a broad consensus among climate scientists that a close correlation exists between the concentration of GHG in the atmosphere and global warming (Intergovernmental Panel on Climate Change, 2018).

The data compiled by the Intergovernmental Panel on Climate Change (IPCC) in its report published in 2014 show that human activity in 2010 generated 49 gigatons (or 49 billion tons) of greenhouse gases in carbon equivalent terms. According to a recent press report, the amount of GHG emitted since then has been estimated at more than 53 billion tons (source: *La Tribune*, November 2019). Many of us would likely struggle to comprehend what that might represent in practice. Consider this: according to the ecoconso.be website, one ton of carbon dioxide equivalent represents a return flight by one person between Brussels and New York (USA) or an 8300 km trip in a small car weighing 1300 kilograms.

Still according to the 2014 IPCC data, current evidence indicates that half of all GHG emissions from human activities since 1750[1] have been generated over the last forty years. Over the period from the 1970s to the 2010s, approximately 80% of emissions are known to have originated

---

[1] The authors of the report acknowledged the arbitrariness of choosing 1750 as the transition year between the pre-industrial and industrial periods.

from fossil fuel combustion and industrial processes. According to the authors of the report, the significant increase in emissions is explained by world population growth and the development of economic activities. World Population Prospects (UN) data indicate that, in 1970, the world's population stood at 3,682,488,000, as compared to 7,349,472,000 in 2015. In other words, the world population has doubled in the space of just 45 years. Alongside population growth, economic development has led to a significant increase in average monthly incomes, with the average income increasing twelve and half fold between 1700 and 2020, representing (in constant value) an increase from 80 to 1000 euros (source: http://piketty.pse.ens.fr/ideologie). In economic development terms, it is easy to see what that might mean in terms of the resources necessary to meet all the needs (see Meadows, Randers, & Meadows, 2004) generated by the doubling of the world population over a period of just 40 years, by comparison with the number of years elapsed since 1750, the date chosen to mark the beginning of the industrial era.

2.1.3   Consequences and Threats

Human industrial activity is known to contribute to the increase in GHG emissions. Their level of concentration in the atmosphere has become a matter of deep concern. Indeed, some of the effects of this concentration are already in evidence. Various examples of the phenomenon are provided below.

For life scientists, one of the most serious effects of the environmental crisis is the collapse of biodiversity. The Zoological Society of London uses the Living Planet Index (or LPI, which measures "the state of global biological diversity based on population trends of vertebrate species from around the world") to provide regular assessments of trends and changes in this area. Its 2018 report pointed to an "overall decline of 60% in the population sizes of vertebrates between 1970 and 2014" (p. 90). An opinion poll published in 2013 by the European Union (entitled "Attitudes towards biodiversity, Flash Eurobarometer 379") revealed that 62% of respondents (26,555 individuals) believe that biodiversity is threatened by climate change, while 78% think that industrial disasters pose a threat. Anecdotally, it is interesting to note that the proportions are generally higher in southern European than in northern European countries. The collapse of biodiversity is a matter of concern to the international community at large. The 2018 report published by the World Wild Foundation

(WWF, 2018) found that the value of the services provided by biodiversity was estimated at USD 125 billion per year. To put it differently, if biodiversity were an imaginary country and if that amount represented the country's total wealth expressed as gross domestic product, the country "Biodiversity" would, according to International Monetary Fund data, have ranked 59th out of 195 countries in 2018 (between and Ukraine and Kuwait). In that sense, biodiversity may be regarded as a significant economic operator.

Other phenomena associated with the effects of climate change include rising sea levels and coastal erosion. In a study published in *Nature Communications*, Kulp and Strauss (2019) found that, depending on the scenario considered (i.e., including or excluding Antarctica) and taking into account the estimated high and low values, somewhere between 140 and 630 million people living in coastal areas will potentially be affected by rising ocean levels by 2050 and undoubtedly by 2100. Rising sea levels are already a reality for a number of island countries, such as the Maldives (source: Lapresse.ca, digital edition of 9 February 2018). In its digital edition of August 27, 2019, *The Guardian* cited the decision of the Indonesian authorities to make serious plans to move the country's capital city more than 1000 km away in response to a whole range of environmental threats, including endemic pollution and flood risks.

The average temperature at the surface of the earth has been increasing constantly in recent years. Heatwaves are becoming increasingly common and ever more intense, and every year that passes is declared to be the hottest on record. The extreme intensity of fires is sometimes identified as one of the collateral effects of this phenomenon.

2.2   International Organizations

There is little doubt that the pressures of human activities are being taken seriously by the international community. They are also being treated (and rightly so) in global and interconnected terms alongside other important topics, such as how to improve the distribution of access to resources, the fight against poverty, and the improvement of the health and well-being of all people (among many other concerns). After World War II, various international organizations were set up with the aim of establishing the necessary social, economic, and political conditions conducive to the emergence of a new global order. The aim was to find a harmonious balance between the socioeconomic needs of a growing population and resource use, with the realization that resources are not only limited but also no longer capable of cyclic regeneration. Without prejudging the matter, it is interesting to note that the efforts of the international community to frame and manage the search for a balance also reveal the limits of their actions. From the earliest manifestos, the role expected of the industrial world has struggled to take shape. Equally, the potential contribution of industry to the overall effort has generally been expressed in relatively vague terms. To a certain extent, this notable absence may explain (but does not justify) the reasons why, globally, industry has tended to keep its distance from the ecological and environmental issues promoted by the international community.

Founded in the late 1960s at the joint initiative of Aurelio Peccei and Alexander King, the Club of Rome was at the origin of the Meadows Report published in 1972 under the title *The Limits to Growth*, in which the authors compiled a large volume of disparate data and achieved the impressive feat of identifying a set of major trends and tendencies. The report discusses the beneficial effects of economic growth, but also the social and environmental pressures to be expected in the event of unbridled growth and development. The updated 2004 edition, in which the authors take stock of the situation roughly thirty years on, highlights the very real benefits associated with the progress made since the publication of the report while also pointing to a number of significant issues. Based on a simple and far from exhaustive lexicographical survey, we find that the terms "enterprises," "firms," "employee," "workforce," "manpower," and "human resources" are seldom used. Indeed, in some cases, they are quite simply missing from the report. The absence of a lexical field traditionally associated with industry is a clear indication that, in the minds of the authors, anthropogenic constraints originate from human activities.

Another example is the Stockholm Declaration. At the initiative of Sweden, the United Nations held the United Nations Conference on the Human Environment in the Swedish capital from 6 to 12 June 1972. The event has come to be known as the Stockholm Conference and is now widely regarded as the first global summit. The resulting declaration is presented in the form of a manifesto designed as a roadmap for the purpose of putting in place a range of concerted measures aimed at ensuring global coordination of efforts to combat environmental degradation. The declaration is in two parts. Part one is written as an 8-point assessment while part two provides a list of 26 principles to be followed. The term "environment" is used more than fifty times throughout the declaration, which is hardly surprising in a text devoted to the environment. Yet there are just four instances associated with industrial activities in the broadest sense. The emphasis placed on the role of industrial activities in environmental deterioration is somewhat limited, even if the fourth observation recognizes that "in the industrialized countries, environmental problems are generally related to industrialization and technology development." The eleventh principle clearly states that the responsibility for correcting the excesses of human activities lies with States and international organizations. Finally, the nineteenth principle aims to promote education for all "in order to broaden the basis for an enlightened opinion and responsible conduct by individuals, enterprises and communities in protecting and improving the environment in its full human dimension." With good reason, the principle banks on knowledge and education as the privileged means of access for promoting widespread environmental awareness. Overall, what emerges from the Stockholm Declaration is that the expectation that industrial operators should contribute to the task of repairing environmental damage remains somewhat superficial—to say the least.

The responsibility for environmental protection would later be taken on by the United Nations Environment Programme (UNEP), and the issue has gradually come to be treated separately from other matters that have given rise to specific programs and led to the creation of dedicated international bodies and nongovernmental organizations. For its part, though not altogether ignored, the role of industry is often largely overlooked. The term "industrial world" is used here in its broadest sense and refers to enterprises, organizations, and firms regardless of their mission, purpose, or type of production. The following section provides some pointers about how organizational activities can impact the environment.

2.3   How Do Organizational Activities Harm the Environment?

2.3.1   Old Issues

There is nothing new about the view of industrial activities as factors of environmental degradation. As already noted, the concentration of GHG in the atmosphere is one of the most significant indicators in this regard. The pressure exerted by industrial activities on the environment coincides closely with the beginning of the industrial revolution in the middle of the eighteenth century. However, a recent study by Preunkert et al. (2019) noted that "lead and antimony appear to be significantly reflective of Roman-era mining and smelting activities" (p. 4958). The results of their study show that releases of pollutants into the environment from human industrial activities appeared well before the industrial revolution. The study provides much food for thought, suggesting that, even at a very small scale, the pollution generated by human activities has long-term effects that are still in evidence 2000 years later.

In the introduction to their paper about the Anthropocene cited above, Crutzen and Stoermer (2000) briefly noted that leading scientists in the nineteenth century were already seeking to understand the relationship between human activities and nature. More recently, in an essay entitled *Natural Interests: The Contest Over Environment in Modern France,* Caroline Ford (2016) showed that, as early as the eighteenth century, the environmental question was a matter of deep concern among enlightened scholars and was already a focus of interest in terms of the effect of excessive resource use on climate change. One example among many others is provided by François Antoine Rauch, a geographer at the Ponts et Chaussées civil engineering authority and the prolific author of a series of studies devoted mostly to the role of forests. As Ford reminds us, Rausch concluded that deforestation "had led to changes in the climate and the seasons, causing violent storms and other environmental anomalies" (p. 53).

2.3.2   Some Contemporary Examples

Organizations can impact the environment in a variety of ways. Of course, the most striking examples are incidents of massive pollution—on the one hand because they have a lasting impact on ecosystems and, on the other, because they represent historical reference points or landmark events. The purpose of the examples provided below is not to cast scorn on the industrial world, not least because an increasing number of businesses are taking ecological matters very seriously by committing to improving their activities with the aim of minimizing their impact on the environment. Indeed, at the micro level, individuals also engage in environmentally harmful behaviors in their everyday life. The key difference is that, at an organizational level, the effects are very visible and involve a far greater capacity for causing environmental damage compared to individual behaviors.

2.3.2.1   Pollution

In the night of 23−24 March 1989, the oil tanker Exxon Valdez ran aground on a rocky bank a few miles off the south coast of Alaska. The tear in the hull resulted in around 40,000 tons of crude oil being discharged along several hundred kilometers of coastline and led to the death of hundreds of thousands of seabirds (Miossec, 2014). The inquiry led by the National Transportation Safety Board cited the human factor (specifically, the ship captain's health) and work organization (the management of night watch shifts) as likely causes for the ship running aground.

Industrial activities generate other forms of pollution that cause harm to the environment, the production and use of plastic being one of the most obvious examples. In the movie *The Graduate* directed by Mike Nichols, Mr. Maguire, a friend of the Robinson family, advises the young Benjamin Braddock, a fresh college graduate played by Dustin Hoffman, to focus on the plastics industry, saying: "Plastics! Think about it. The great future is in plastics." The story takes place in the late 1960s. The character's lines, though uttered in a fictional work, are borne out by the development of the plastics industry in real life. An extremely comprehensive study conducted by Geyer, Jambeck and Law (2017) on the matter provides some dizzying statistics. In the 1950s, the annual production of plastic in the form of resin and fiber totaled around two million tons. By 2015, production had increased to 380 million tons. The authors also note that a total of 7800 million tons of plastic have been produced since 1950, half of which has been produced since the beginning of the 2000s, indicating exponential growth. At the same time, the total volume of plastic waste has been increasing constantly. The build-up of plastic waste is partly associated with industrial practices and the durability of plastic, which, depending on the use made of it, varies between one year in the case of packaging to 10 years when used in the construction industry. The authors of the study also estimated that 60% of the plastic produced since the 1950 s has ended up in nature understood in the broadest sense, i.e., in landfills and oceans. The resulting build-up is all to the detriment of the natural world. In its report entitled *No Plastic in Nature: A Practical Guide for Business Engagement*, the World Wild Foundation noted that "environmental damage to marine ecosystems, meanwhile, is estimated to be USD 13 billion per year" (p. 9).

2.3.2.2 Transport

Modern human activities are to a great extent governed by transport, with commuting representing a major factor. Megalopolises such as New York City and Tokyo see millions of people traveling to their place of work every day. For many of them, public transport is the preferred commuting mode. However, commuting alone by car remains the most common method of transport. In 2017, approximately 4,800,000 people commuted each day into New York City (Source: U.S. Census Bureau, 2017 American Community Survey), with most commuters using public transport (2,800,000 people). A quarter of all commuters travel alone in their own car (representing slightly more than 1,000,000 people), while just 200,000 people use carpooling.

In addition, a UK-based environmental organization (AirportWatch), which describes itself as "an umbrella movement networking the interested environmental organisations, airport community groups, and individuals opposed to unsustainable aviation expansion, and its damaging environmental effects, including climate change, noise and air pollution," estimated in a 2011 report (Lockley, 2011) that approximately 4% of global GHG emissions were attributable to air transport.[2]

2.3.2.3 Digitalization

Digitalization is the central issue of our times. The concept refers to a wide range of practices often seen as extensions of human labor. Smartphones, tablets, and connected devices have become common work tools supplementing the good old computer. A careful observer might watch the actions and practices of customer-facing employees as they use such tools to obtain information in real time (stock status, delivery time, order taking, online payment, etc.). Though small if taken in isolation, each consultation or request contributes to pollution.

In the same vein, it is estimated that 230 billion emails (including personal and work emails) are sent each day (source: *Madame Figaro*, 8 November 2019). One email generates approximately 20 grams of CO_2 (source: ADEME.fr). As part of their daily work, employees commonly use messaging services to communicate with members of their organization or with external partners (whether customers or suppliers). It is

---

[2] In this regard, Lockley indicated that "[t]he estimate published for the GWP(100) was 1.9−2.0, suggesting that a multiplier of 2 applied to CO2 emissions is justified on a precautionary basis to account for the non-CO2 effects of aviation" (p. 15).

also common to receive messages in the form of distribution lists, which may also include attachments. For the same sender, a practice such as this considerably increases the sources of pollution as a result of the combined CO2 emissions produced by each email and each attachment sent (source: Digital for the Planet). Finally, the estimated annual environmental cost of using email as a means of communication in a work setting in a company with 100 employees is approximately 14 tons of carbon equivalent (source: https://www.arobase.org/actu/chiffres-email.htm), representing, again, 14 Brussels-New-York return flights.

Finally, it has become increasingly common to see wording at the bottom of emails inviting recipients to print only when necessary. There is no doubt that using such wording underlines the sender's concern for the environment and that consulting documents electronically to avoid printing has the benefit of limiting the use of paper. Yet while this may be a commendable practice in theory, in reality it only serves to displace the ecological footprint issue. What it conceals is the vast infrastructure required to ensure that a simple click is all it takes for a recipient to receive the message addressed to them almost instantaneously. Data centers are key components of this infrastructure. Their chief function is to provide the necessary computing power and to enable data storage, and they are notoriously energy-intensive. According to recent estimates, their annual consumption accounts for around 4% of global energy consumption (source: www.planetoscope.com). Based on a recent estimate of the total annual emission of GHG, this represents around 2.1 gigatons of CO2 equivalent each year.

Though highlighting and recognizing the key role of human activities since the advent of large-scale industrialization, the few examples cited above say little about the role of individuals from the point of view of their subjectivity in a work setting.

2.4   What About Individuals at Work?

The greening of workplaces cannot be examined without considering the key role of employees.

Environmental issues in organizational settings cover a wide range of topics, from waste management to the establishment of environmental standards within organizations (known as ISO 14001 standards) and industrial risk management. A significant proportion of the related literature addresses the role of the various stakeholders involved in the decision of an organization to adopt industrial process management practices that take into account environmental constraints. By limiting the focus to regular members of the organization, the literature has tended to focus primarily on the implications of decision-making by top management and the upper echelons of management. On the whole, the literature has largely overlooked the key role of employees. My point is not that studies devoted to the role of employees in the greening of workplaces are nonexistent. Indeed, over the last decade, a dynamic research stream has emerged in this area. However, it remains a marginal stream when compared to topics studied at the organizational and managerial levels.

Mobilizing with the same degree of intensity employees with different levels of environmental awareness around principles of environmental responsibility is a major challenge for the greening of workplaces. Organizational units bring together individuals with varying levels of personal interest in environmental issues, ostensibly diverging ecological values and conflicting perceptions of the challenges associated, for example, with global warming. It has been noted that the greening of organizations and, therefore, of workplaces requires effort and commitment on the part of all employees at all organizational and hierarchical levels (Paul & Nilan, 2012). However, the evidence shows that employees may not necessarily take a personal interest in ecological matters and, beyond these, in the social problems raised by environmental issues (Paillé, Rainerim, & Boiral, 2019). Differences in the level of environmental awareness are one known aspect—but an aspect that is often neglected, in my view, in the specialized literature. On the assumption that the preservation of the natural environment is an end largely rooted in a moral perspective of responsibility to future generations, it cannot be assumed that all people not only understand the urgency but also demonstrate a high level of environmental commitment in their daily work.

Some concluding remarks

That being said, two final questions deserve attention: Are green employees always consistent? And can they really be consistent? In my classes and lectures, I often recount the same anecdote to illustrate how difficult it is for us, as individuals, to always act in accordance with the ideas and values that we uphold, sometimes vigorously so. One winter's day, one of my colleagues (who will remain unnamed to spare his blushes) suggested, as he often did, that we go off campus for lunch. In his day-to-day work, my colleague rarely printed documents, preferring instead to read them on screen, and made a conscious choice to continue using his IT equipment so long as it met all his requirements. He would also often put into practice the observations and findings yielded by his research. Yet, having arrived at one of the entrances to our department building, he stopped, removed a gadget in the form of a keyring from his coat pocket and pointed the device toward the parking lot located approximately a hundred meters away. Intrigued, I asked what he was doing, to which he simply replied: "I'm using the remote starter." The gesture might have gone unnoticed if it had been performed by anyone other than my colleague, who happens to be an influential researcher with an interest in environmental issues in his field of study.

What this anecdote invites us to think about are the difficulties surrounding the consistency of ecological actions and behaviors at an individual level. The fact of not behaving in accordance with one's pro-environmental beliefs can be explained in several ways. The context plays a particularly important role. In the situation described above, the rigors of winter were experienced as a sufficiently significant constraint for ecological considerations to be relegated to a secondary plane. The anecdote also challenges the degree of persistence of individual ecological considerations in time and in space. The arguments set out in the next chapters will help to improve our understanding of these issues.

REFERENCES

Crutzen, P. J., & Stoermer, E. F. (2000). The "anthropocene", global change. *NewsLetter, 41*, 17–18.

Ford Caroline. (2016). *Natural interests. The contest over environment in modern France*. Cambridge: Harvard University Press.

Geyer, R., Jambeck, J. R., & Law, K. L. (2017). Production, use, and fate of all plastics ever made. *Science Advances, 3*(7), 1–5.

Intergovernmental Panel on Climate Change (2018). The Special Report on Global Warming of 1.5 °C (SR15).

Kulp, S. A., & Strauss, B. H. (2019). New elevation data triple estimates of global vulnerability to sea-level rise and coastal flooding. *Nature Communications, 10*(1), 1–12.

Lockley, P. (2011, July). *Aviation and climate change policy in the UK*.

Meadows, D., Randers, J., & Meadows, D. (2004). *Limits to growth: The 30-year update*. Vermont, USA: Chelsea Green Publishing.

Miossec, A. (2014). *Géographie des mers et des océans*. PUR: Rennes.

Paillé, P., Raineri, N., & Boiral, O. (2019). Environmental behavior on and off the job: A configurational approach. *Journal of Business Ethics, 158,* 253–268.
Paul, K. B., & Nilan, K. J. (2012). Environmental sustainability and employee engagement at 3M. In S. E. Jackson, D. S. Ones, & S. Dilchert (Éds.), *Managing human resource for environmental sustainability* (pp. 267–280). Wiley: Jossey-Bass.
Preunkert, S., McConnell, J. R., Hoffmann, H., Legrand, M., Wilson, A. I., Eckhardt, S., … Friedrich, R. (2019). Lead and antimony in basal ice from Col du Dome (French Alps) dated with radiocarbon: A record of pollution during antiquity. *Geophysical Research Letters, 46*(9), 4953–4961.
WWF. (2018). *Living planet report 2018: Aiming higher* (N. Grooten & Almond REA, Eds.). WWF, Gland, Switzerland.

CHAPTER 3

Employee Environmental Behaviors

Abstract This chapter provides a review of current knowledge on pro-environmental behaviors in organizations. A classification based on the following 4 characteristics will be proposed: the type of behavior, the degree of inclusion in work tasks, the required intensity, and the type of position held. The main methods used in the study of employee environmental behavior are also discussed.

Keywords Definition · Classification · Operationalization · Methods

3.1 Definition, Classification and Concept

3.1.1 Main Conceptual Definitions

In one of the first critical literature reviews to be published on the drivers of pro-environmental behaviors (PEBs) in organizations, Lo, Peters, and Kok (2012) emphasized the wide variety of concepts used in research on how employees behave responsibly toward the environment. My own overview of the literature indicates that, since this first review, the study of specific behaviors has not only grown dramatically but has also led to a proliferation of terms used to classify specific behaviors in distinct categories. While some scholars have opted to use the term "organizational citizenship behavior for the environment" (Paillé, Boiral, & Chen,

2013), others prefer to speak of "PEBs," (Zibarras & Coan, 2015) "corporate greening behavior," (Ramus & Killmer, 2007) "employee green behavior," (Norton, Parker, Zacher, & Ashkanazy, 2015) or "environmental workplace behaviors" (Ciocirlan, 2017). The range of competing concepts and definitions found in the literature is simply a reflection of the depth and richness of this field of study, despite its relative infancy.

The sheer variety of concepts used in this area raises several questions: does the terminology currently in use reflect semantic choices aimed at locating and defining the different disciplinary fields of management and environmental psychology in relation to one another? Do the terms used refer to different constructs designed to account for a specific environmental reality? Given the wide range of concepts involved in the study of environmental issues in organizational settings, an interesting challenge is to determine the extent to which they overlap or differ. I propose to draw a connection between them by using the definitions provided by the promoters of the concepts as a point of reference. Figure 3.1 provides a visual representation of the matter.

Ramus and Killmer (2007) argued that "corporate greening behaviours are best conceived of as prosocial organizational behaviours" (p. 556). They also argued that most employees tend not to view such behaviors as required tasks. The idea broadens the discussion to a wider question about the extent to which environmental issues are included in work tasks, the aim being to explicitly determine whether a given environmental behavior should be viewed in in-role or extra-role terms. This view is shared by Mesmer-Magnus, Viswesvaran, and Wiernik (2012), who argued that "pro-environmental behaviors encompass all individual behaviors that contribute to environmental sustainability" (p. 169).

Other definitions are more inclusive since they propose to include both individual actions aimed at protecting the environment and behaviors that are potentially harmful to the environment. Ones and Dilchert (2012b) adopted a broader view, using the concept of "employee green behavior" defined as "scalable actions and behaviors that employees engage in that are linked with and contribute to or detract from environmental sustainability" (p. 87). More recently, Ciocirlan (2017) introduced the notion of environmental workplace behaviors, defined as "work behaviors directed toward the protection or improvement of the natural environment, which may or may not generate value for the organization; these behaviors may be performed by employees situated at any organizational level" (p. 56).

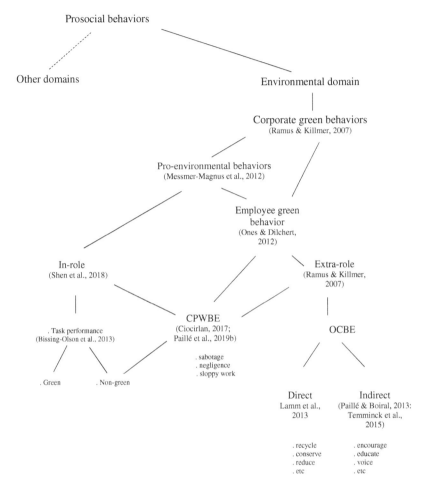

Fig. 3.1 Suggested links between concepts

The concept of organizational citizenship behaviors for the environment (OCBE) is explicitly rooted in the literature on organizational citizenship behaviors. In that sense, the notion of OCBE may be viewed as an explicit extension and application of the concept of citizenship behaviors to the environmental domain. The extension is explicit in the sense that, in their conceptualization, items are clearly oriented toward individual positions or views with respect to environmental matters. Interestingly, one of the founding texts of organizational citizenship research (Bateman & Organ, 1983) suggests that questions relating to the environment in the broadest sense are implicit. For example, the authors note that "[t]he items tapped a variety of behaviors such as compliance, altruism, dependability, housecleaning, complaints, waste, cooperation, criticism of and arguing with others, and punctuality" (p. 589). While it is objectively difficult to make any assumptions about the authors' intentions, and without wishing to overinterpret their arguments or findings, the topics of housecleaning and waste may be said to be in some sense connected to, or to fall within the remit of, ecological and environmental questions.

However, these similarities are more explicitly apparent in two papers published by Daily, Govindarajulu, and Bishop (2009) and Boiral (2009). Daily et al. (2009) proposed to define OCBEs as "discretionary acts by employees within the organization not rewarded or required that are directed toward environmental improvement" (p. 246), while Boiral and Paillé (2012) defined OCBE as "individual and discretionary social behaviours that are not explicitly recognized by the formal reward system and that contribute to a more effective environmental management by organizations" (p. 431). These definitions involve three key elements of organizational citizenship behavior: the discretionary, voluntary, and performative nature of environmental behaviors in work settings. The following pages will seek to develop complementary approaches while examining OCBE in different forms, including individual behavioral intentions aimed at participation, support, and encouragement to adopt green behaviors (Boiral, 2009; Boiral and Paillé, 2012), practical individual actions toward the environment (recycling and energy saving) (Lamm, Tosti-Kharas, & Williams, 2013), suggestions, voicing, and the dissemination of ideas relating to the environment (Temminck, Mearns, & Fruhen, 2015). Though still only nascent in many respects, the literature devoted to organizational citizenship behaviors for the environment now appears to have reached a stage where it may be able to emancipate itself from the research framework governing the study of organizational citizenship behaviors.

The dotted arrow indicates that, when departing from a strictly environmental framework, pro-environmental behaviors only represent one form of individual engagement among others.

3.1.2   Main Eco-Friendly Behaviors in the Workplace

The topic of eco-friendly behaviors in the workplace is now a well-documented issue. While several typologies have been developed to address the issue, the most complete and accomplished work carried out to date is the typology involving employee green behaviors (Ones & Dilchert, 2012b), which has been used as the basis for a significant number of studies in the field (Francoeur, Paillé, Yuriev, & Boiral, 2019; Norton et al., 2015). Depending on the case at hand, the typology includes a varying number of environmental behaviors around the five categories defined by Wiernik et al. (2016: p. 5). The number of subcategories has been further refined in recent research, as illustrated, for example, by Francoeur et al. (2019), who proposed "to consider environmental civic mindedness, environmental voice behavior, and performing sustainable daily work as subcategories of taking initiatives, influencing others, and transforming, respectively" (p. 20).

- Conserving (recycling, reusing, reducing, repurposing): "behaviors aimed at avoiding wastefulness and preserving resources."
- Avoiding Harm (pollution monitoring, environmental impact, strengthening ecosystems, choosing responsible alternatives): "Behaviors involving avoidance and inhibition of negative environmental behaviors."
- Working Sustainably (Changing how work is done, creating sustainable products and processes, embracing innovation for sustainability, performing sustainable daily work): "behaviors aimed at enhancing the environmental sustainability of work products and processes."
- Influencing Others (Educating and training for sustainability, encouraging and supporting others, initiating programs and policies, environmental voice behavior): "Behaviors aimed at spreading sustainability behaviors to other individuals"
- Taking Initiative (Lobbying and activism, putting environmental interests first, environmental civic mindedness): "Behaviors which involve pro-actively initiating new behaviors or making personal sacrifices for sustainability."

Based on a review of forty years of research on environmental practices at the individual level in the workplace, Francoeur et al. (2019) also found that behaviors relating to the category "conserving" have received considerable attention compared to behaviors belonging to the categories "avoiding harm" and "transforming," a finding consistent with the results of another study (Yuriev, Dahmen, Paillé, Boiral, & Guillaumie, 2020). The literature also shows that recycling is the most widely studied individual behavior. Environmental research has shown that employees routinely engage in recycling practices in their workplace, such as paper recycling (Lamm et al., 2013), glass, plastic, and aluminum recycling (Stritch & Christensen, 2016), recycling of electronic components (Manika et al., 2015), food waste recycling (Mak et al., 2018), and industrial waste recycling (Li, Zuo, Cai, & Zillante, 2018). However, it is important to note that the use of the term 'recycling' is an abuse of language. When a person disposes of paper or food in the appropriate container or places a plastic object in the right bin, he or she cannot be said to be engaging in recycling per se. At best, what that person is doing is contributing to one of the many stages of waste collection, sorting, and disposal. Collecting, sorting and disposing of waste are merely the preliminary stages of a much broader process involving numerous parties in a lifecycle of varying length depending on the type of product in question.

3.2   Outlining How Employees Behave Toward the Environment

3.2.1   Green vs Nongreen Behaviors

An individual's decision to work for, or to seek for work in, an organization genuinely committed to promoting ecological and environmental matters demonstrates a degree of individual awareness of environmental issues. In other words, understanding environmental behavior requires a joint consideration of the sector or industry in question, the environmental or ecological mission or intentions of the organization, and the type of position held within the organization.

3.2.1.1   Industrial Level
An important factor to consider is whether an employee works for a company operating in a green or nongreen industry, which may sometimes take the form of a traditional industry (Ones and Dilchert 2012a). The notion of green industry refers to "those sectors that adopt cleaner production technology as well as harmless or less harmful new technology" (Hu, 2017). By contrast, the notion of nongreen industry

corresponds to "industries with large consumption of resources and heavy environmental pollution" (Wei, Yuguo, & Jiaping, 2015). A word of caution is needed here. Taken literally, both definitions may appear to suggest that businesses can be distinguished along somewhat Manichean lines, with environmentally responsible companies contrasting with environmentally careless companies.

In actual fact, the distinction between a green industry and a nongreen industry is somewhat artificial since the fact of belonging to one or the other is based on the subordination of the organization's commercial and industrial activities to a range of environmental practices, rules and standards, such as a code of environmental ethics, environmental policy, product and process stewardship, and environmental management systems (Lober, 1996). The fact that an organization belongs to a green industry implies that it takes its duty to minimize its environmental impact seriously. Organizations in this category tend to forge commercial and industrial links with partners exhibiting, if not the same concerns, at least operational management procedures conforming, in theory, to a range of normative constraints evidenced by appropriate environmental accreditations or standards. By contrast, an organization that belongs to a nongreen industry will tend to incorporate such concerns in its commercial and activities only to a very limited extent. While this may suggest that the activities of a nongreen organization are less subject to normative regulation at an environmental level, it should not be assumed that representatives of the organization have no concern for environmental matters. Indeed, environmental certifications and standards can create their own constraints and restrictions in terms of application, access costs, and lack of necessary organizational resources (see Chapter 7).

3.2.1.2 Job Level

Similarly, a distinction is sometimes made between green and nongreen jobs. Providing a clear definition of these concepts is no easy task, contrary to what a naïve understanding of the concept of green job might suggest. In "Response to 'Seven Myths about Green Jobs' and 'Green Jobs Myths,'" Pollin (2009) provides a range of explanations, underlining the difficulty of conceptualization. As Pollin notes: "we face serious problems in attempting to establish a single operational definition of the term green jobs." For example, if a truck driver is delivering solar panels to a construction site, should that count as a "green job?" What if, the next day, the same truck driver delivers pumping equipment to an offshore oil drilling project? Even within the project to install solar panels on rooftops, we would of course consider the electricians and roofers doing the installation as having green jobs. But what about the secretaries and accountants in the back office? (p. 3). More recently, Bowen (2012) suggested that the difficulty of defining the concept of green job can be explained by the sheer variety of approaches used by researchers, who have generally tended to adopt a sector-based approach rather than an approach focused on the job or position held. Having considered several definitions, Bowen concluded that solving an environmental problem is less ecological than preventing it. What may appear to be a tautology raises, in my view, a crucial problem for greening the workplace. Ultimately, it is not the job itself that is green but the substance of the daily actions of the individual holding that job and, by extension, the nature of their professional activities. Put differently, the characteristics associated with a job provide employees with the means to behave in environmentally responsible ways. The implication is that a distinction must be made between the job and the person holding and performing that job.

3.2.1.3   Individual Level

Does a person who has a green job really behave responsibly toward the environment? Similarly, does the fact of having a traditional job (as opposed to a green job) mean that a person is highly irresponsible? It would be misleading to infer a person's level of environmental engagement from their job. In my view, we need to think carefully about what criteria should be used to determine whether an employee is green or not green. Ciocirlan (2017) found that some employees within an organization are more concerned than others about environmental issues. Within an organization, three groups of employees coexist and can be distinguished according to the degree to which they have incorporated environmental matters as part of their professional identity. Rather like Russian dolls, the three groups overlap. The largest group includes all employees, i.e. both those with little interest in or concern for environmental matters and those with a high level of interest and concern. The group of employees with a limited interest in environmental matters should not be assumed to be a group containing nongreen employees since that would imply that they voluntarily adopt environmentally questionable behaviors (see Chapter 4). In the case of nongreen employees, environmental matters are simply not a part of their everyday habits and are not incorporated into their daily work routines.

According to Ciocirlan (2017), green employees are more likely than other employees to report a prominent, salient, and committed environmental identity (p. 54), have an intrinsic motivation to protect the environment at work (p. 55), and display similar levels of comparable environmental behaviors between home and work settings (p. 55). Among the green employee subgroup, some commit compulsively to the environment while others, though concerned with environmental matters, appear to show less interest. The degree of intensity with which employees engage in environmental issues can be used as a basis for categorizing employees into two groups: employees who exhibit high-intensity engagement and employees who exhibit low-intensity engagement. The difference is determined by the degree to which environmental concerns shape and direct an individual's actions on a daily basis. High intensity indicates that ecology and the environment are ingrained in an individual's identity. Each action is invariably shaped by environmental concerns. By contrast, in the case of low intensity, environmental concerns exist but do not systematically shape or direct individual action on a daily basis. In other words, in such situations, an individual is able to adapt to behavioral breaches that do not cause significant disruption to their identity. The usefulness of the distinction will be discussed in due course (see Chapter 8).

The green/nongreen criterion suggests that we may view the question of greening the workplace from a broader perspective. In fact, crossing (non)green job with (non)green industry and (non)green individuals creates numerous possibilities. The purpose here is not to discuss the implications arising from every possible combination. Nonetheless, it is easy to see the scale of the environmental and human challenges that a business must face it if is to become more environmentally friendly by adopting operational practices that adhere to ecological standards (e.g., production processes designed to minimize waste) and/or by adopting environmental standards (e.g., ISO 14000). Ones and Dilchert (2012a) argued that the formal requirements of a job in a green industry are more likely to encompass environmental matters when compared to traditional industries, where, more often than not, employees will simply be encouraged to behave responsibly toward the environment, a requirement not specifically referred to in their job description.

3.2.2   Inclusion in the Job Task

In itself, the idea of distinguishing a job task by considering the degree of inclusion of a particular concern (health, safety, service, etc.) is not new. What is new is the attention paid to environmental considerations. To the best of my knowledge, Ramus and Killmer (2007) were among the first to classify environmental behaviors based on the in-role/extra-role distinction. With a few rare exceptions, environmental behaviors are for the most part seen as extra-role behaviors (Francoeur et al., 2019). In other words, the implication is that their degree of inclusion in job tasks is particularly low. Put differently, employee engagement in practical pro-environmental actions and behaviors is to a large extent voluntary and driven by a deep personal belief in the importance of behaving pro-environmentally.

The most fruitful discussions in this area have taken the degree of inclusion into account by introducing the notions of "in-role" and "extra-role". Since the pioneering study of Katz and Khan (1966), the distinction between in-role and extra-role has become well established and is now widely accepted. Ziegler and Schlett (2016) defined in-role behavior as "actions which are expected to be carried out by employees because of formal job descriptions and role assignments" (p. 2), whereas, according to Miller, Rutherford, & Kolodinsky (2008), extra-role behavior "involves the execution of acts not necessarily described in a job description" (p. 212). The distinction between in- and extra-role tasks creates a grey area: where does an in-role task end and an extra-role begin? This is not a new question. The aim is to establish what is meant in practice by a required action or behavior in a work setting. What is a required behavior? When does a behavior cease to be required? Providing a general answer to this question is no easy task. The degree of requirement is closely linked to the type of job held. A required behavior is, by nature, constraining because it directs the actions and efforts of an individual and determines what must be done within a given time and space. The difficulty of establishing exactly where formal demands and requirements begin and end may have something to do with the fact that it is sometimes difficult to clearly distinguish the job from the role to be performed (Organ, 1997). We may posit that a behavior ceases to be required when an individual is required to deliberate with themselves or others in order to facilitate the course of action related to that behavior.

Following Ramus and Killmer (2007), Bissing-Olson, Iyer, Fielding, and Zacher (2013) were among the first to consider the idea of the inclusion of tasks for empirical purposes, defining "task-related pro-environmental behavior as the extent to which employees complete their required work tasks in environmentally friendly ways" (p. 157). In their approach, the authors view task-related pro-environmental behavior as discretionary individual behaviors. This nuance is important. Unlike the related literature relating to job performance and, more specifically, to minimum expected efficiency in task performance (Motowidlo, 2003), employees cannot really be sanctioned if they fail to consider or largely neglect environmental concerns in their daily tasks. In addition, Bissing-Olson et al. (2013) proposed that "[t]ask-related pro-environmental behavior takes place within the context of employees' required core work tasks, whereas proactive pro-environmental behavior moves outside these narrow parameters and involves a more active, change-oriented, and self-starting approach to environmental issues in the workplace" (p. 158). Ultimately, what this suggests is that, even in workplace settings, environmental concerns remain confined to the individual level from the point of view of intentionality and that they cannot be explicitly included within the sphere of required behaviors, implying that the effectiveness of environmental concerns ultimately lies in their degree of routinization in work tasks.

More recently, Shen, Dumon, and Deng (2018) defined nongreen task performance as "nongreen behavior-related tasks that are required within a job role, which are essential employee workplace behaviors that contribute to improving organizational efficiencies and effectiveness" (p. 597). Here, such behaviors are viewed as not falling under the category of green behaviors, which is very different from treating them as nongreen behaviors. Here, the term "nongreen" is misleading since it appears to suggest that the behaviors examined in their study relate to behaviors that fall under the category of nongreen individual actions, whereas the aim was to examine behaviors that clearly refer to in-role and extra-role behaviors in the form of organizational citizenship behavior and intention to quit the organization.

A study by Francoeur et al. (2019) on the operationalization of environmental behaviors established that, for the most part, the studies conducted in this area between 1977 and 2018 focus on extra-role environmental behaviors, while those examining intra-role behaviors account for a much smaller proportion (4.5%). On this point, the findings concerning methodological efforts are consistent with those reported in conceptual literature reviews (e.g., Ciocirlan, 2017; Norton et al., 2015; Ones & Dilchert, 2012a).

3.2.3   Direct vs Indirect Environmentally Friendly Behaviors in the Workplace

To the best of my knowledge, the distinction between direct and indirect behaviors was first introduced by Homburg and Stolberg (2006). An environmentally friendly behavior is defined as direct when an individual engages personally in pro-environmental behavior by taking practical action to contribute to waste avoidance, pollution reduction, and the minimization of excessive resource use. By contrast, an environmentally friendly behavior is defined as indirect when an individual engages in actions designed to encourage members of their organization to understand environmental issues with a view to them adopting responsible behaviors. In that sense, indirect environmental behaviors may be seen as a means to an end.

Indirect environmental behaviors can act as drivers of direct pro-environmental or anti-environmental behaviors. It seems reasonable to suggest that encouragements made by an employee with high environmental awareness may cause colleagues with little interest in environmental matters to gradually alter their day-to-day environmental habits. Equally, the support provided by an employee recognized for their know-how in the form of a symbolic recognition of environmental efforts made may, by extension, encourage other colleagues to engage in environmentally responsible behaviors through a mimetic effect. Environmentally concerned employees can also educate and train colleagues open to learning about simple environmental practices and habits. It seems realistic to envisage that environmental employee voice behaviors can contribute to the dissemination of environmental ideas by triggering a new awareness that has the potential to promote the emergence of an environmental culture in the workplace that is conducive to the adoption of direct environmental behaviors.

3.2.4   Further Considerations

The first consideration is the degree to which employees are capable of differentiating between different behaviors. The question may seem trivial, but it was given serious consideration in a January 2008 report by the Department for Environment, Food and Rural Affairs (Defra), as the following excerpt makes clear: "The Defra scoping report set out the early development of a segmentation model, which is a critical tool in the framework for influencing behaviour. As has already been intimated, different people act (or not) for different reasons; a motivation for one may well be a barrier for another" (p. 40). The report focuses mainly on environmental behaviors performed outside organizational settings. Yet this line of thinking is also relevant to the study of environmental behaviors in organizational settings. Understanding whether employees view environmental actions and behaviors as a whole or are capable of making clear distinctions between different behaviors is important from an academic point of view, but also matters for practical reasons—not least because the question serves to extend thinking on the levers of organizational and managerial action designed to encourage employee environmental engagement. Several empirical studies have shown that employees distinguish clearly between different environmental behaviors, whether these relate to direct behaviors such as recycling and energy saving (Gregory-Smith, Wells, Manika, & Graham, 2015) or indirect behaviors such as environmental helping, environmental civic mindedness, or individual initiatives (Boiral & Paillé, 2012).

Lastly, one final point is the broader question of the degree to which environmental behaviors overlap or are interconnected. The behavioral sequence refuse → reduce → reuse → recycle situates pro-environmental behaviors in relation to each other based on their degree of environmental impact. The sequence is itself part of a broader sequence involving nine stages and goes beyond the strict confines of individual actions and behaviors in the workplace (on this subject, see a 2017 study by Kirchherr, Reike and Hekkert in which the authors examined definitions of the notion of "circular economy"). In theory, while refusing to consume resources to minimize the carbon footprint may be the most pro-environmental behavior (as rightly noted by Ones and Dilchert), recycling is the least environmentally friendly action since it requires the use of additional energy resources to complete the treatment process. In a workplace setting, and strictly from an employee point of view, refuse behavior is nonetheless difficult to mobilize. Furthermore, a lack of consideration for the waste generated by daily work activities is simply inconceivable for reasons of health, safety, and hygiene in shared spaces within an organization. Refuse behavior is one possible option under certain conditions. It may take a specific form whereby employees limit excessive resource use as far as they can, exhibited in the form of reduction behavior. Reduce can take different forms and may also involve different purposes through targeted behaviors. Energy consumption reduction can be achieved through specific actions such as turning off lights when leaving the office or when not needed, using double-sided printed or photocopied documents, turning off computer monitors when not in use, and the use of video conferencing rather than traveling to meetings (Dixon, Deline, McComas, Chambliss, & Hoffmann, 2015; Greaves, Zibarras, & Stride, 2013; Lamm et al., 2013). Waste reduction is another possible reduction strategy (Tudor, Barr, & Gilg, 2008). For example, employees can be encouraged to bring their own mug to work to avoid using a new Styrofoam cup when they drink coffee.

3.3 EMPLOYEE GREEN BEHAVIORS AND THEIR OPERATIONALIZATION

3.3.1 Overview

Considerable efforts have been made in recent years to operationalize environmental behaviors. A study by Francoeur et al. (2019) based on a systematic literature review provides an illuminating insight into the choices made over the years in this area. Their study is based on a sample of 53 papers published between 1977 and 2019.[1] According to Francoeur et al. (2019):

- 46 of the 53 papers (87%) are based on a quantitative approach (using Likert-type measurement scales);
- 7 of the 53 papers (13%) used a qualitative approach (i.e. experimentation and/or direct observations).

Francoeur et al. (2019) showed that the operationalization of pro-environmental behaviors is largely dominated by quantitative approaches involving, for the most part, the use of measurement scales. Fewer studies on pro-environmental behaviors have been conducted from a global or

[1] See Francoeur et al. (2019) for methodological details.

comprehensive perspective. In what follows, I provide a brief description of these different options.

3.3.2 Quantitative Approaches

The term "quantitative approach" is understood to mean the use of data acquisition methods allowing for analysis based on measurement operations (mean, standard deviation, etc.). Based on Francoeur et al. (2019), two indications of interest are worth noting here. First of all, the first measurement scale used in an organizational context for research on environmental behaviors appeared in1994 in a paper by Lee and De Young. Second, 22 measurement scales were published between 1994 and 2019, giving a total of 170 items. The items are distributed as follows:

- 60% relate to direct behaviors;
- Measurement typically focuses on extra-role rather than in-role behaviors;
- Conserving behaviors are mostly operationalized (47.65%);
- New subcategories have emerged, including (a) performing sustainable daily work, (b) environmental civic mindedness, and (c) environmental voice behavior.

The list of available items is particularly long, suggesting the need for a considered assessment. The aim is to drastically reduce the redundancies between different scales so as to ensure that future studies use a more consistent approach for operationalizing pro-environmental behaviors in the workplace.

By way of example, I propose to extract items referring to the category "reuse".[2] Several comments can be made about the resulting list. Reuse as a behavior is included in 7 different measurement scales, giving 12 items in total. Three topics are addressed. They are:

Container reuse:

- Use reusable bottles or cups for beverages (Stritch & Christensen, 2016).

---

[2] Readers interested in all the scales and how items are distributed according to the category to which they belong are referred to Francoeur et al. (2019).

- I am a person who uses a reusable water bottle instead of a paper cup at the water cooler or faucet (Lamm et al., 2013).
- I am a person who uses a reusable coffee cup instead of a paper cup (Lamm et al., 2013).
- I use my own cup instead of disposable ones (Chou, 2014).
- I use a mug for drinking coffee/tea (Blok, Wesselink, Studynka, & Kemp, 2015).
- Using personal cups instead of disposable cups (Kim, Kim, Han, Jackson, & Ployhart, 2017).
- I take a new plastic/carton cup each time I have coffee or tea (reverse) (Blok et al., 2015).

The use of reusable utensils:

- I bring reusable eating utensils to work (e.g., travel coffee mug, water bottle, reusable containers, reusable cutlery) (Robertson & Barling, 2013).
- I carry my own chopsticks instead of using disposable ones (Chou, 2014).

Paper reuse:

- I am a person who uses scrap paper for notes instead of fresh paper (Lamm et al., 2013).
- Reusing papers to take notes in the office (Kim et al., 2017).
- Use the unused side of paper for notes, messages, and copies (Lee & Young, 1994).

These items involve unique scenarios. It is clear from the above that the emphasis is primarily on container reuse. The focus here is implicitly on reducing the use of single-use containers such as plastic and paper cups for water and hot drinks. Finally, very little consideration is given to paper reuse behavior in a work context—a surprising fact when considering, for example, the number of items in measurement scales that involve paper recycling in one form or another (more than 10 items distributed across 7 scales between 1994 and 2016).

3.3.3 Case Study

Dumitru et al. (2016) used the case study approach in order, on the one hand, to examine the factors that affect energy use in work-related behavior and, on the other, to understand the motivational bases driving employees to behave pro-environmentally. Two case studies were carried out (one in a Spanish university and another in an Italian energy company). The case study method allows observers to access a wide range of data related to the subject under study. Dumitru et al. analyzed and compared data obtained from multiple sources, including websites, brochures, promotional and advertising flyers, organization charts, environmental and social reports, and codes of ethics, supplemented by a series of in-depth interviews of key informers (high-level management staff in relevant positions). The case study approach provides a broader and more detailed understanding of the phenomenon under study made possible by a detailed analysis of the studied context, but also imposes many constraints on researchers. Case study research is, by its very nature, contingent, considerably limiting the potential for replicating the study and for generalizing the results.

3.3.4 Experimental Design

Several studies in this area have used an experimental design approach in varying forms. In this type of approach, one of the preferred practices involves using one or more scenarios. The underlying principle involves presenting subjects with hypothetical scenarios controlled by the researcher. The advantage of experimental design is that scenarios can be manipulated in order to refine the basis of the analysis. A good example is Bohlmann, van den Bosch, and Zacher (2018), who used this method to determine the extent to which employees in managerial positions tend to incorporate environmental behaviors alongside other traditional behaviors (mutual support, deviant behaviors) as a general criterion for assessing their subordinates' overall performance. The main details of the experimental apparatus are as follows. Scenarios combining several behavioral statements referring to individual behaviors were developed. The scenarios were presented to the study participants, who were then asked to grade them. The main results were as follows. Like any methodological apparatus, an experimental study provides benefits but also suffers from various shortcomings. The main benefit is that, in experimental research, the observed effect can be isolated by neutralizing the contextual contingencies that typically affect field studies. The flipside of that benefit is that, by its very nature, experimentation implies an artificial context which, regardless of its heuristic value, limits the practical scope and significance of observation.

3.3.5   Situated Experiment

Gregory-Smith et al. (2015) tested two environmental social marketing interventions on several types of behaviors (recycling, printing, and heating/cooling). To do so, the authors used a situated experimental approach. The intervention was designed to raise employee awareness of the value of adopting a responsible attitude toward the use of paper and air conditioning. The awareness-raising process involved using both general visual communication (i.e., posters) and direct personalized communication (i.e., email). Measurements of pro-environmental attitudes and behaviors pre- and post-intervention were performed. The situated experimentation method broadly involves transferring the general principles of laboratory experimentation to a real-world setting (i.e., a British City Council). The advantage of this approach is that it avoids the objections commonly leveled against out-of-context experimental approaches, which have been criticized primarily for the artificiality of the resulting observations and the difficulty of generalizing the results. Gregory-Smith et al. (2015) acknowledged various limitations largely related to the fact that some of their data were second-hand, making it impossible to establish the effectiveness of the intervention on certain aspects (in particular, no measurement was performed prior to the intervention on employees' attitudes toward environmentally friendly behavior in the workplace).

3.3.6   Mixed Methods

Researchers opting to use qualitative approaches generally tend to combine several different methods. A good example is the study conducted by Humphrey, Bord, Hammond, and Mann (1977) on employees' environmentally sustainable behavior in the context of resource conservation (i.e., manual separation of wastepaper in offices). The study combined direct observation of individual behaviors with quantitative measures. Another example is the study by Scherbaum, Popovich, and Finlinson (2008) on energy-saving behaviors in the workplace, in which the authors combined the focus group technique and the questionnaire method. Using several techniques enables researchers to draw on the benefits associated with each method used, but also introduces a degree of constraint in terms of the extraction and analysis of raw data and the interpretation of results obtained from different sources.

Some concluding remarks

The scope of this chapter was limited to presenting various key aspects of the core focus of this book, such as key definitions, the main structuring characteristics, and the different modes of operationalization. Judging by the number of papers published on the subject in the last decade, the question of environmental behaviors is a thriving area of research. Drawing on the above, employees may be said to behave in eco-friendly ways in the workplace when they engage in conscious, discrete, voluntary, (in)direct and intentional actions with the explicit goal of protecting the environment or of harming it as little as possible. Behaviors that potentially detract from environmental matters also need to be considered. This is the topic of the next chapter.

REFERENCES

Bateman, T. S., & Organ, D. W. (1983). Job satisfaction and the good soldier: The relationship between affect and employee "citizenship". *Academy of Management Journal, 26*(4), 587–595.

Bissing-Olson, M. J., Iyer, A., Fielding, K. S., & Zacher, H. (2013). Relationships between daily affect and pro-environmental behavior at work: The moderating role of pro-environmental attitude. *Journal of Organizational Behavior, 34*(2), 156–175.

Blok, V., Wesselink, R., Studynka, O., & Kemp, R. (2015). Encouraging sustainability in the workplace: A survey on the pro-environmental behaviour of university employees. *Journal of Cleaner Production, 106*, 55–67.

Bohlmann, C., van den Bosch, J., & Zacher, H. (2018). The relative importance of employee green behavior for overall job performance ratings: A policy-capturing study. *Corporate Social Responsibility and Environmental Management, 25*(5), 1002–1008.

Boiral, O. (2009). Greening the corporation through organizational citizenship behaviors. *Journal of Business Ethics, 87*(2), 221–236.

Boiral, O., & Paillé, P. (2012). Organizational citizenship behaviour for the environment: Measurement and validation. *Journal of Business Ethics, 109*(4), 431–445.

Bowen, A. (2012). *Green'growth,'green'jobs and labor markets.* The World Bank.

Chou, C. J. (2014). Hotels' environmental policies and employee personal environmental beliefs: Interactions and outcomes. *Tourism Management, 40,* 436–446.

Ciocirlan, C. E. (2017). Environmental workplace behaviors: Definition matters. *Organization & Environment, 30*(1), 51–70.

Daily, B. F., Bishop, J. W., & Govindarajulu, N. (2009). A conceptual model for organizational citizenship behavior directed toward the environment. *Business and Society, 48*(2), 243–256.

Defra. (2008). Department for Environment, Food and Rural Affairs. Sustainable Clothing Roadmap Briefing Note. December 2007 (updated March 2008).

Dixon, G. N., Deline, M. B., McComas, K., Chambliss, L., & Hoffmann, M. (2015). Saving energy at the workplace: The salience of behavioral antecedents and sense of community. *Energy Research & Social Science, 6,* 121–127.

Dumitru, A., De Gregorio, E., Bonnes, M., Bonaiuto, M., Carrus, G., Garcia-Mira, R., et al. (2016). Low carbon energy behaviors in the workplace: A qualitative study in Italy and Spain. *Energy Research & Social Science, 13,* 49–59.

Francoeur, V., Paillé, P., Yuriev, A., & Boiral, O. (2019). The measurement of green workplace behaviors: A systematic review. *Organization & Environment.* https://doi.org/10.1177/1086026619837125.

Greaves, M., Zibarras, L. D., & Stride, C. (2013). Using the theory of planned behavior to explore environmental behavioral intentions in the workplace. *Journal of Environmental Psychology, 34,* 109–120.

Gregory-Smith, D., Wells, V. K., Manika, D., & Graham, S. (2015). An environmental social marketing intervention among employees: Assessing attitude and behaviour change. *Journal of Marketing Management, 31*(3–4), 336–377.

Homburg, A., & Stolberg, A. (2006). Explaining pro-environmental behavior with a cognitive theory of stress. *Journal of Environmental Psychology, 26*(1), 1–14.

Hu, A. (2017). Green Enterprise Innovation. In *China: Innovative Green Development* (pp. 159–185). Singapore: Springer.

Humphrey, C. R., Bord, R. J., Hammond, M. M., & Mann, S. H. (1977). Attitudes and conditions for cooperation in a paper recycling program. *Environment and Behavior, 9*(1), 107–124.

Katz, D., & Kahn, R. L. (1966). *The social psychology of organizations.* New York: Wiley.

Kim, A., Kim, Y., Han, K., Jackson, S. E., & Ployhart, R. E. (2017). Multi-level influences on voluntary workplace green behavior: Individual differences, leader behavior, and coworker advocacy. *Journal of Management, 43*(5), 1335–1358.

Kirchherr, J., Reike, D., & Hekkert, M. (2017). Conceptualizing the circular economy: An analysis of 114 definitions. *Resources, Conservation and Recycling, 127,* 221–232.

Lamm, E., Tosti-Kharas, J., & Williams, E. G. (2013). Read this article, but don't print it: Organizational citizenship behavior toward the environment. *Group and Organization Management, 38,* 163–197.

Lee, Y. J., & De Young, R. (1994). Intrinsic satisfaction derived from office recycling behavior: A case study in Taiwan. *Social Indicators Research, 31*(1), 63–76.

Li, J., Zuo, J., Cai, H., & Zillante, G. (2018). Construction waste reduction behavior of contractor employees: An extended theory of planned behavior model approach. *Journal of Cleaner Production, 172,* 1399–1408.

Lo, S. H., Peters, G. J. Y., & Kok, G. (2012). A review of determinants of and interventions for proenvironmental behaviors in organizations. *Journal of Applied Social Psychology, 42*(12), 2933–2967.

Lober, D. J. (1996). Evaluating the environmental performance of corporations. *Journal of Managerial Issues, VIII*(2), 184–205.

Mak, T. M., Iris, K. M., Tsang, D. C., Hsu, S. C., & Poon, C. S. (2018). Promoting food waste recycling in the commercial and industrial sector by extending the Theory of Planned Behaviour: A Hong Kong case study. *Journal of Cleaner Production, 204,* 1034–1043.

Manika, D., Wells, V. K., Gregory-Smith, D., & Gentry, M. (2015). The impact of individual attitudinal and organisational variables on workplace environmentally friendly behaviours. *Journal of Business Ethics, 126,* 663–684.

Mesmer-Magnus, J., Viswesvaran, C., & Wiernik, B. M. (2012). The role of commitment in bridging the gap between organizational sustainability and environmental sustainability. In Jackson, S. E., Ones, D. S., & Dilchert, S. (Eds.), *Managing human resources for environmental sustainability* (Vol. 32). San Francisco, CA: John Wiley & Sons.

Miller, B., Rutherford, M., & Kolodinsky, R. (2008). Perceptions of organizational politics: A meta-analysis of outcomes. *Journal of Business and Psychology, 22*(3), 209–222.

Motowidlo, S. (2003). Job performance. In W. Borman, D. Ilgen, R. Klimoski, & I. Barrick (Eds.), *Handbook of psychology* (pp. 39–52). New York, NY: Wiley.

Norton, T. A., Parker, S. L., Zacher, H., & Ashkanasy, N. M. (2015). Employee green behavior: A theoretical framework, multilevel review, and future research agenda. *Organization & Environment, 28*(1), 103–125.

Ones, D. S., & Dilchert, S. (2012a). Environmental sustainability at work: A call to action. *Industrial and Organizational Psychology, 5*(4), 444–466.

Ones, D. S., & Dilchert, S. (2012b). Employee green behaviors. In Jackson, S. E., Ones, D. S., & Dilchert, S. (Eds.), *Managing human resources for environmental sustainability* (Vol. 32). San Francisco, CA: John Wiley & Sons.

Organ, D. W. (1997). Organizational citizenship behavior: It's construct clean-up time. *Human Performance, 10*(2), 85–97.

Paillé, P., Boiral, O., & Chen, Y. (2013). Linking environmental management practices and organizational citizenship behaviour for the environment: A social exchange perspective. *The International Journal of Human Resource Management, 24*(18), 3552–3575.

Pollin, R. (2009). *Response to "Seven Myths about Green Jobs" and "Green Jobs Myths"* (PERI Working Paper 198). Amherst, USA: University of Massachusetts.

Ramus, C. A., & Killmer, A. B. (2007). Corporate greening through prosocial extrarole behaviours–A conceptual framework for employee motivation. *Business Strategy and the Environment, 16*(8), 554–570.

Robertson, J. L., & Barling, J. (2013). Greening organizations through leaders' influence on employees' pro-environmental behaviors. *Journal of Organizational Behavior, 34*(2), 176–194.

Scherbaum, C. A., Popovich, P. M., & Finlinson, S. (2008). Exploring individual-level factors related to employee energy-conservation behaviors at work 1. *Journal of Applied Social Psychology, 38*(3), 818–835.

Shen, J., Dumon, J., & Deng, X. (2018). Employees' perception of Green HRM and non-green employee work outcomes: The social identity and stakeholders' perspectives. *Group & Organization Management, 43*(4), 594–622.

Stritch, J. M., & Christensen, R. K. (2016). Going green in public organizations: Linking organizational commitment and public service motives to public employees' workplace eco-initiatives. *American Review of Public Administration, 46,* 337–355.

Temminck, E., Mearns, K., & Fruhen, L. (2015). Motivating employees towards sustainable behaviour. *Business Strategy and the Environment, 24*(6), 402–412.

Tudor, T. L., Barr, S. W., & Gilg, A. W. (2008). A novel conceptual framework for examining environmental behavior in large organizations: A case study of the Cornwall National Health Service (NHS) in the United Kingdom. *Environment and Behavior, 40*(3), 426–450.

Wei, Z., Yuguo, J., & Jiaping, W. (2015). Greenization of venture capital and green innovation of Chinese entity industry. *Ecological Indicators, 51,* 31–41.

Wiernik, B. M., Dilchert, S., & Ones, D. S. (2016). Age and employee green behaviors: A meta-analysis. *Frontiers in Psychology, 7,* 194.

Yuriev, A., Dahmen, M., Paillé, P., Boiral, O., & Guillaumie, L. (2020). Pro-environmental behaviors through the lens of the theory of planned behavior: A scoping review. *Resources, Conservation and Recycling, 155,* 104660.

Zibarras, L. D., & Coan, P. (2015). HRM practices used to promote pro-environmental behavior: a UK survey. *The International Journal of Human Resource Management, 26*(16), 2121–2142.

Ziegler, R., & Schlett, C. (2016). An attitude strength and self-perception framework regarding the bi-directional relationship of job satisfaction with extra-role and in-role behavior: The doubly moderating role of work centrality. *Frontiers in Psychology, 7,* 235.

CHAPTER 4

The Question of Non-Environmental Behaviors

Abstract This chapter aims to refine our understanding of the key issues surrounding the greening of workplaces by focusing on non-environmental behaviors. The question of non-environmental behaviors has been little studied and remains poorly understood. Although rare, studies in this area suggest that individuals may adopt non-environmental behaviors in their workplace without intending to cause harm to the natural environment or even without realizing that their actions are environmentally harmful. The aim will be to provide the basis for drawing a fine distinction between environmental and non-environmental behaviors.

Keywords Non-environmental behaviors · Individual intention · Counterproductive behaviors · Operationalization

4.1 Defining the Issue of Non-environmental Behaviors

4.1.1 The Nature of the Problem

While it is relatively easy to picture what a green behavior might look like, it is probably more difficult to imagine precisely what a nongreen behavior might amount to. This question has been given relatively little attention in the academic literature. Nonetheless, the small number of field studies

© The Author(s) 2020
P. Paillé, *Greening the Workplace*,
https://doi.org/10.1007/978-3-030-58388-0_4

conducted in this area, as well as the documented facts and available evidence, suggest that nongreen behaviors are, in fact, far more common than we may think. Within a relatively confined space (e.g. an administrative division) over a short period of time (a day's work), a careful observer could easily identify a wide range of inappropriate actions and behaviors when examining work situations from an environmental perspective.

A good example of nongreen behavior might involve taking the elevator rather than the stairs to talk to a colleague whose office is located on the floor immediately above one's own. Other examples include not using double-sided printing and using online searching, while leaving the office at the end of the day without switching off one's computer would obviously count as environmentally unfriendly behavior. There are many other examples. Taken in isolation, behaviors such as these may seem harmless at the individual level and may even be regarded as common instances of oversight. However, when considered from the perspective of the organization as a whole, they may be seen as the reflection of a work context in which individuals care little about environmental matters.

In another register, some actions and behaviors appear to be indicative of a different attitude or state of mind. Let us consider two examples. Each year, ships are caught in the act of illegal deballasting and dumping at sea. Cleaning out and deballasting are operations that should be carried out in confined spaces and environments. Illegal deballasting (or degassing) involves emptying tanks and ballasts containing oily waste and oil residue at sea (source: https://la1ere.francetvinfo.fr). Likewise, many businesses in the paper mill and foundry industries are often singled out for discharging pollutants such as lead and arsenic into rivers. Similar criticisms are routinely leveled against the water treatment plans of certain city councils for discharging ammonia in wet areas (source: Radio-Canada, 7 November 2015).

Though incomparable in one respect, ordinary carelessness and more dubious behaviors represent two distinct categories of situations that are nonetheless comparable from the point of view of their impact on the environment. In dealing with this type of behavior, the question we need to ask is whether it involves a decision that reflects a profound lack of environmental awareness or an intention to harm the environment. In the first case, we might be more inclined to speak of a lack of care or concern, while in the second case the problem is best viewed in terms of environmentally irresponsible practices. A key factor here is intention. Discharging chemical products into a river cannot be said to fall under the category of environmentally irresponsible behavior if the cause relates to a technical fault that cannot be attributed to a malicious intent or attitude. The difference is a matter of scale. The choice of terminology will tend to locate the two behaviors on different scales of assessment in terms of environmental harm and the scale of the impact.

4.1.2   Definition

The term "irresponsible environmental behavior" is sometimes used to describe potentially harmful individual actions. Though widely recognized, the principle of irresponsibility in an environmental context has rarely been defined, and there has been relatively little discussion of the substance of the principle. Okereke, Vincent, and Mordi (2018) proposed to define irresponsible environmental behavior as the opposite of responsible environmental behavior, defined as the perceived likelihood of a manager engaging in actions and decisions that are environmentally friendly (p. 581). However, the authors do not define irresponsible environmental behavior. The implication is that irresponsible behavior in environmental terms derives from individual actions and decisions that are not environmentally friendly, a proposition that suggests the need to distinguish between an action and a decision.

Environmentally irresponsible behavior can be analyzed in several ways. An irresponsible act is defined as an act performed by a person who fails to see the incongruity of their actions in the act of performing them. An irresponsible act is also an action whose immediate and longer-term impact has either not been anticipated or has simply been ignored. A lack or absence of anticipation can be explained by the fact that it is often simpler and less costly to behave irresponsibly rather than responsibly in relation to a cause calling for much moral deliberation (Ohtomo & Hirose, 2007). The most common explanation for justifying irresponsible behaviors is ignorance (see Chapter 8). An analysis in terms of irresponsibility therefore implies considering both the action or behavior itself and its consequences. Disposing of plastic packaging in an organic waste container is a good example of clumsiness or inattention that has effects beyond the act itself. This example has a number of implications. For example, it undermines the principle of organic waste recycling in that it imposes an additional requirement for waste sorting. However, an irresponsible action or behavior may not necessarily be motivated by a malicious intent to harm the environment. In some cases, such behaviors can simply be explained by a lack of understanding of what should be done in a given situation. Here, irresponsibility appears to be more attributable to a lack of knowledge or ignorance and less attributable to an intention to cause deliberate harm to the environment.

In seeking to understand the inappropriateness of an environmental behavior, the first question that arises is this: At what point can a behavior be said to be non-environmental? This seemingly simple question implies another, which may seem somewhat impertinent: Can a workplace really be pro-environmental? Here, it is all a matter of defining what we mean by "workplace" and "pro-environmental." It is also a matter of defining precisely what we mean by the limits or boundaries of the workplace. For example, a person traveling for business may be said to be extending the boundaries of their workplace. What this suggests is that we need to rethink the scope of (non)environmental behaviors associated with work tasks. A person traveling for business has an impact on the environment regardless of their chosen mode of transport. However, they will have a greater or lesser impact depending on the mode of transport they choose and the distance traveled (see Chapter 9).

The pro-environmental behavior of organizations is sometimes reflected by their employees' personal attitudes. Depending on the terminology used, researchers speak of environmental voice behavior or environmental lobbying (Francoeur, Paillé, Yuriev, & Boiral, 2019). A good example is provided by journalists working at the Danish daily newspaper *Politiken*. As well as a range of measures aimed at reducing the carbon footprint, the newspaper's editorial board recently decided to put an end to all business trips by plane. In fact, choosing not to fly to attend a meeting several hundred miles away and using videoconferencing instead appears, on the face of it, not only to be environmentally friendly, but is also more productive from an economic point of view and indeed less onerous from a human point of view. However, when considering environmental matters specifically, it should be noted that replacing one practice with another does not reduce the carbon footprint of the replacement activity to zero. Indeed, to assume that it does would be to deceive oneself. For the same activity—in this case, attending a meeting—the carbon footprint is very real in both cases. However, compared to air travel, videoconferencing has a smaller impact on the environment. Yet some estimates shed a different light on the actual environmental impact of flying when considered alongside other realistic modes of transport in a given situation. Comparative analyses of CO2 emissions suggest the need to rethink a number of deeply rooted preconceptions. According to Bernet (2018), in the case of distances of around 1000 km, one person emits almost the same amount of GHG when traveling by air and road. When traveling twice that distance, driving generates around a third more emissions compared to flying. What the comparison shows is that, in all cases, traveling by train is the most effective way of reducing GHG emissions. In short, opting not to fly for work reasons is a pro-environmental behavior rooted in a personal decision, though choosing to drive can prove to be a non-environmental choice.

At first glance, it seems reasonable to assume that not behaving responsibly toward the environment should be interpreted differently by taking into account both the nature of job tasks and the type of industry. Thus, refraining from performing a sustainable act may be interpreted as an environmentally irresponsible behavior in a green industry, whereas in a traditional industry it may only be perceived as a lack of concern. Likewise, according to the degree of inclusion in the task, the same behavior can be classified as an irresponsible act if environmental concerns are inherent to the work undertaken (in-role behavior) or as a simple oversight if such concerns only fall within the scope of desirable behaviors (extra-role behavior). A contextualized approach is vital for capturing the nuances necessary for an in-depth analysis of nongreen behaviors.

4.2   Counterproductive Environmental Behavior

Nongreen behaviors can be classified in the category of counterproductive behaviors—a category that is the subject of an abundant literature. Behaviors falling within this category are sometimes studied in terms of organizational or interpersonal deviance.

Here, we need to refer back to the classic definition given by Robinson and Bennett (1995), who proposed to define counterproductive behavior as an act "that violates significant organizational norms and in so doing threatens the well-being of an organization, its members, or both" (p. 556). Based on this definition, a counterproductive act may be said to be directed against either the organization or its members and may be defined as a minor or major instance. Robinson and Bennett provide a list of 45 behaviors drawn from evidence obtained in the course of their investigation. These behaviors provide a useful inclusive model. Some examples of deviant actions included in the list are given below by way of providing a more detailed picture of how such behaviors are typically categorized.

Examples of minor deviant actions directed toward the organization (referring to product deviance) include:

- Leaving work early;
- Taking long breaks;
- Working slowly;
- Wasting resources.

Examples of major deviant actions directed toward the organization (referring to property deviance) include:

- Sabotaging equipment;
- Lying about hours worked;
- Thefts of equipment;
- Accepting corruption.

Examples of minor deviant acts directed toward members of the organization (referring to political deviance) include:

- Playing favorites;
- Slandering colleagues;
- Sterile competition;
- Gossip.

Examples of major deviant acts directed toward members of the organization (referring to personal aggression) include:

- Harassment;
- Insult;
- Stealing from colleagues;
- Putting colleagues in danger.

Regardless of the target and scale of the act, the approach taken by Bennett and Robinson introduces the principle of intent to harm. It is important to take intention into account since doing so provides a means of distinguishing such behaviors from inappropriate behaviors reflecting faux-pas or blunders that may be explained, for example, by a lack of interpersonal skills.

To the best of my knowledge, and except for the example referring to wasting organizational resources provided by Robinson and Bennett, Ciocirlan (2017) was the first to examine the question of nongreen behaviors from the perspective of counterproductive behaviors. The value of this approach lies in how counterproductive environmental behavior is conceived since it proposes to shift the perspective by adopting the employer's viewpoint rather than the employee's.

The scenario considered by Ciocirlan involves an employee complaining about their employer's actions. When an organization takes decisions or commits acts that violate moral principles or when it devises strategies that are not consistent with environmental values advocated for commercial purposes and these practices are publicly denounced by one or more members, the latter are generally identified as disloyal. Green behavior is thus perceived as counterproductive from the employer's perspective since it deviates from the principle of loyalty as the employer sees it. In this case, it would appear to be the way in which the employer defines loyalty that requires attention, not the deviation of the behavior from such loyalty. In this view, green behavior is counterproductive from the point of the employer and not the employee. If we consider things from an employee perspective while acknowledging the degree of professional risk associated with the fact of revealing potentially harmful organizational situations at the environmental level, an employee may legitimately assume that he or she is acting in a civic and responsible manner. It will be the decisions and actions of other members of the organization that will be described as instances of counterproductive environmental behavior. The examples of degassing and pollutant discharge given at the beginning of this chapter may be said to fall under the category of counterproductive non-environmental behaviors.

By examining insubordination behaviors in terms of counterproductive environmental behavior, Ciocirlan shifts the focus of attention by placing individuals in the category of whistleblowers, thereby offering a new perspective that helps to broaden our understanding of the studied phenomenon. However, in doing so, it is important to acknowledge that Ciocirlan does not consider the case of environmental malevolence at the individual level. The argument can be extended by examining situations in which individuals come, through their actions, to adopt behaviors that are harmful to the environment. Two perspectives based on the intentional nature of the act merit consideration. A counterproductive behavior will convey different messages depending on whether it is intentional or not. This is an important nuance. As noted previously, counterproductive behaviors carry a meaning that generally directs the analysis toward negative or harmful behaviors. Robinson and Bennett (1995) noted that an "employee intentionally making errors" is a form of counterproductive behavior capable of disrupting work processes and, depending on the scale of the error, of impacting the safety of facilities and colleagues. Overall, errors at work are not sought by those who make them on account of the professional discomfort that they can create (Bauer, 2008). In short, making deliberate mistakes sends a strong signal and places employees in an unambiguous stance toward their workplace. Making such a choice is consistent with the principle of intentionality referred to previously.

However, errors at work may also reflect an altogether reality. Paillé, Morelos, Raineri, & Stinglhamber (2019) proposed to examine non-environmental behaviors as a softer form of sloppy work simply because environmental behaviors have been found at times to be based on habits and routines acquired in the past. As the flow of work unfolds day after day, ingrained habits and routines can lead to imperceptible and unconscious gaps that may detract from environmental sustainability over time (Lamm, Tosti-Kharas, & Williams, 2013). This is precisely what led Paillé et al. (2019) to argue that "inappropriate environmental acts performed by individuals in their daily work, such as wasting energy, may therefore merely be a reflection of a lack of environmental concern at work without any purposeful intention per se to harm the natural environment. In this regard, lack of engagement may simply be caused, for instance, by a disregard for the environment as an important issue, insufficient knowledge, selfishness or lack of reflection on the consequences of one's actions" (p. 725).

Describing nongreen behavior as a form of counterproductive behavior has significant implications since it involves ascribing a deliberate intent to harm the environment to the individual committing the act. This raises the question of how to interpret the meaning of individual actions aimed at intentionally harming the environment. If we refer back to the main criteria provided by Robinson and Bennett in their definition, what is required is a deliberate transgression of norms that causes harm to the organization or its members (depending on the type of act).

The application of this idea (and of the associated research framework) to environmental issues requires a degree of adaptation that presupposes viewing nature as a stakeholder. As noted previously, the debate around Nature as a stakeholder is far from over. At present, it seems premature to even provide the beginnings of an explanation. It may be worth exploring another avenue. Based on recent developments, we may approach the subject from another angle. In the management literature, counterproductive behavior is a means to an end. An employee chooses singular behavior as a means of expressing their frustration. If we take this view, harming the environment may also be thought of in terms of a means to an end. However, in this case, the intent to harm is not directed toward the environment, which is merely a catalyst.

In the examples given above, we saw that resource wasting is viewed as a minor deviant act directed toward the organization and is defined as a form of productive deviance. In this case, if resources such as electricity (turning on the air conditioning and opening the windows at the same time), water (leaving the taps on when exiting the restroom) and paper are wasted with the intention of generating additional costs for the organization, it seems sensible to suggest that the environment is impacted, but only indirectly so. Through these practices, the organization is targeted more directly than the environment. In this case, we may speak of sabotage. Sabotage is the subject of a vast literature and is generally the result of an individual response to a deep sense of injustice stemming from an accumulation of frustrating experiences (Ambrose, Seabright, & Schminke, 2002).

The practice of resource wasting was described above as a form of behavior aimed at sabotaging the conditions for achieving environmental performance. The next study I propose to discuss is a very interesting example of a means to an end. Focusing on the civil aviation industry, Harvey, Williams and Probert (2013) examined how individual actions related to industrial sabotage can affect environmental performance. After providing various contextual details related to the aviation industry that are prone to cause tension at work, Harvey et al. focused their analysis on flight crew and, specifically, on airline pilots—a focus explained by the significant degree of autonomy afforded by their role. Their study highlighted the discretionary decisions that are sometimes made by pilots in response to managerial practices with which they disagree. For example, choosing a longer flightplan, deciding to fly at a higher altitude and increasing the amount of fuel onboard are sometimes deliberate choices intended to increase GHG emissions. Intentional actions such as these have repercussions for the financial sanctions imposed on airline companies that fail to comply with their industry's emission standards. This study provides a perfect illustration of the means-to-an-end principle.

4.3   How Can Nongreen
Behaviors Be Operationalized?

Nongreen behaviors have been operationalized in different ways. For example, Ones and Dilchert (2012) used the critical incidents method developed by Flanagan in the 1950s. As a qualitative method, the technique involves freely recalling individual experiences and is based on the underlying idea of starting from a situation experienced by an individual rooted in a specific context in order to categorize their attitudes and behaviors in relation to an object of study. Like all methods, the critical incidents technique provides various benefits (e.g., richness and depth of corpus), but also has a number of disadvantages (e.g., cognitive biases).

The specialized literature also includes modes of operationalization associated with quantitative methods. Measurement scales tend to be the preferred method for investigating nongreen behaviors. Examples include attempts at operationalization in the form of dedicated measurement scales and items involving singular non-environmental situations in measurement scales directed more broadly toward general environmental behaviors (see Francoeur et al., 2019).

The items listed below are associated with different measurement scales. The scenarios envisaged view nongreen behaviors from very different perspectives, whether in terms of level of priority, allocated time, or other factors. The various items are also associated with different levels of perception. For example, the first two items relate to employees in management positions, while the remaining four items concern nonmanagerial employees.

- I refuse to commit resources and employee time for training and education in environmental issues (Andersson, Seabright, & Schminke, 2005);
- I complain about additional work resulting from environmental practices (Alt & Spitzeck, 2016);

- In my workplace, environmental protection has to take second place behind other obligations (Homburg & Stolberg, 2006);
- In my daily work, I forget to carry out environmental protection measures (Homburg & Stolberg, 2006);
- I tend to print emails for ease of reference (Manika et al., 2015).

Unlike the above list, the list of items provided below is associated with the same measurement scale (Paillé et al., 2019). The scale was used once, providing good psychometric properties. It presents advantages in terms of internal consistency (Cronbach's alpha = .76; composite reliability = .85).

- I rely on technology to solve environmental problems at work, it's not my business;
- At work, I let others worry about environmental protection;
- I do not apply environmental standards that could slow my pace of work;
- In my workplace, I do not care about the consumption of water or electricity;
- In my work, I ask my collaborators and colleagues to prioritize productivity and not the environment;
- Whenever I have the chance, I tell my coworkers that environmental behaviors are a waste of time.

In summary, the environmental literature has given serious consideration to non-environmental behaviors at the methodological level. However, these initial forays require their operationalization to be further refined.

4.4   How Are Nongreen Behaviors Linked to Green Behaviors?

The study of nongreen behaviors raises the question of their relationship with green behaviors. To what extent does behaving in an environmentally friendly or unfriendly way reflect two sides of the same coin? For example, is the fact of not recycling the opposite behavior to recycling paper? This question merits attention since its theoretical implications are vital for understanding how employees act toward the environment in a work environment.

Ones and Dilchert (2013) argued that while employees may behave in an environmentally responsible way in their daily work, they are also prone to make decisions or to act in ways that contradict their environmentally responsible interests. Their survey showed that a significant proportion of actions (between 18 and 25% according to their observations) could be described as nongreen actions at work. The study highlights an interesting point, which is that the percentage provided does not relate to the proportion of people involved but the proportion of clumsy or inappropriate actions committed: rather than suggesting that one in five *people* undertakes nongreen actions, the study found that one in five *actions* are nongreen. The distinction is important since it implies that the same person may perform green behaviors in some circumstances but act irresponsibly in other circumstances. The theoretical and practical implications of this question will be discussed at a later stage when examining obstacles to the adoption of green behaviors.

Another interesting point worth mentioning relates to the conceptualization of nongreen behaviors. In various publications (2012, 2013), Ones and Dilchert suggested that the same green behavior, whatever it may be, can be viewed from two different angles. The positive side refers to an environmentally friendly action at work, while the negative side reflects the opposite—i.e., an environmentally harmful action. The distinction can be illustrated based on one of the authors' own examples drawn from the category of "initiative-taking" behavior. In a work setting, prioritizing environmental interests may reflect environmentally responsible behavior (for example, not using too much air conditioning in warm weather) or demonstrate environmentally irresponsible behavior (for example, not wanting to compromise one's own comfort at work by refusing to reduce the amount of energy consumed through using an air-conditioning unit). However, beneficial or harmful actions are not treated as discrete behaviors but as poles of the same behavior viewed, in their most extreme form, as opposite behaviors along the same continuum. This issue raises the conceptual problem of the point of equilibrium at which an individual behaves in neither an environmentally friendly nor an environmentally unfriendly manner and is hypothetically located equidistantly from the positive and negative poles. Though hypothetical, this scenario challenges the very foundations of the continuum principle. Green and nongreen behaviors may be viewed as discrete variables that are conceptually related but empirically distinct. At the time of writing, no empirical studies had yielded results along these lines. However, based on the parent literature and, in particular, the results of Dalal (2005), it seems reasonable to posit the idea of common behavioral grounds.

Some concluding remarks

This chapter sets out to describe a common but largely neglected reality: the existence of non-environmental behaviors. The general idea defended in this chapter was that it is wrong to view non-environmental behaviors as voluntary actions since they may simply be the reflection of carelessness or oversight. Ultimately, if we adhere to the definition of employee green behavior, the implication is that we need to consider both the positive polarities formed by environmental citizenship behaviors, whether in their direct (Lamm et al., 2013) or indirect forms (Boiral and Paillé, 2012), and the negative polarities, sometimes termed irresponsible environmental behaviors or counterproductive environmental behaviors. However, as discussed, the principle of positive and negative polarities implies an empirical impasse that cannot be resolved with the idea of environmental inaction, which itself reflects the situations described by Tanner (1999) under the term Ipsative Theory in order to formalize cases in which individuals are faced with a lack of alternatives for acting in an environmentally responsible manner (see Chapter 8).

REFERENCES

Alt, E., & Spitzeck, H. (2016). Improving environmental performance through unit-level organizational citizenship behaviors for the environment: A capability perspective. *Journal of Environmental Management, 182,* 48–58.

Ambrose, M. L., Seabright, M. A., & Schminke, M. (2002). Sabotage in the workplace: The role of organizational injustice. *Organizational Behavior and Human Decision Processes, 89*(1), 947–965.

Andersson, L., Shivarajan, S., & Blau, G. (2005). Enacting ecological sustainability in the MNC: A test of an adapted value-belief-norm framework. *Journal of Business Ethics, 59*(3), 295–305.

Bauer, J. (2008). *Learning from errors at work. Studies on nurses' engagement in error-related learning activities* (Doctoral dissertation).

Bernet, C. (2018). https://www.24heures.ch/economie/bilan-carbone/story/23861440.

Boiral, O., & Paillé, P. (2012). Organizational citizenship behaviour for the environment: Measurement and validation. *Journal of Business Ethics, 109*(4), 431–445.

Ciocirlan, C. E. (2017). Environmental workplace behaviors: Definition matters. *Organization & Environment, 30*(1), 51–70.

Dalal, R. S. (2005). A meta-analysis of the relationship between organizational citizenship behavior and counterproductive work behavior. *Journal of Applied Psychology, 90*(6), 1241–1255.

Francoeur, V., Paillé, P., Yuriev, A., & Boiral, O. (2019). The measurement of green workplace behaviors: A systematic review. *Organization & Environment.* https://doi.org/10.1177/1086026619837125.

Harvey, G., Williams, K., & Probert, J. (2013). Greening the airline pilot: HRM and the green performance of airlines in the UK. *The International Journal of Human Resource Management, 24*(1), 152–166.

Homburg, A., & Stolberg, A. (2006). Explaining pro-environmental behavior with a cognitive theory of stress. *Journal of Environmental Psychology, 26*(1), 1–14.

Lamm, E., Tosti-Kharas, J., & Williams, E. G. (2013). Read this article, but don't print it: Organizational citizenship behavior toward the environment. *Group and Organization Management, 38*(2), 163–197.

Manika, D., Wells, V. K., Gregory-Smith, D., & Gentry, M. (2015). The impact of individual attitudinal and organisational variables on workplace environmentally friendly behaviours. *Journal of Business Ethics, 126*(4), 663–684.

Ohtomo, S., & Hirose, Y. (2007). The dual-process of reactive and intentional decision-making involved in eco-friendly behavior. *Journal of Environmental Psychology, 27*(2), 117–125.

Okereke, C., Vincent, O., & Mordi, C. (2018). Determinants of Nigerian managers' environmental attitude: Africa's Ubuntu ethics versus global capitalism. *Thunderbird International Business Review, 60*(4), 577–590.

Ones, D. S., & Dilchert, S. (2012). Employee green behaviors. In Jackson, S. E., Ones, D. S., & Dilchert, S. (Eds.), *Managing human resources for environmental sustainability* (Vol. 32). San Francisco, CA: John Wiley & Sons.

Ones, D. S., & Dilchert, S. (2013). Measuring, understanding, and influencing employee green behaviors. In *Green organizations: Driving change with IO psychology* (pp. 115–148). New York: Routledge.

Paillé, P., Morelos, J. H. M., Raineri, N., & Stinglhamber, F. (2019). The influence of the immediate manager on the avoidance of non-green behaviors in the workplace: A three-wave moderated-mediation model. *Journal of Business Ethics, 155*(3), 723–740.

Robinson, S. L., & Bennett, R. J. (1995). A typology of deviant workplace behaviors: A multidimensional scaling study. *Academy of Management Journal, 38*(2), 555–572.

Tanner, C. (1999). Constraints on environmental behaviour. *Journal of Environmental Psychology, 19*(2), 145–157.

CHAPTER 5

Theoretical Approaches

Abstract The chapter presents social exchange theory and describes its value for the study of environmental sustainability in organizational settings when the focus is on the individual. The chapter also reviews various related research areas with the aim of identifying synergies and takes stock of the different theories that have been used in the environmental literature to establish differences and convergences.

Keywords Social exchange theory · Related research areas · Theoretical approaches

5.1 Social Exchange: A New Theoretical Approach for Environmental Sustainability

5.1.1 Definition, Key Premises and Core Principles

5.1.1.1 Theoretical Foundations

A decade ago, Steg and Vlek (2009) argued that "the conditions under which a particular theory is most successful in explaining environmental behaviour need more attention" (p. 315). Regardless of its foundations, a theory provides a means of understanding the subject at hand. Bell, Greene, Fisher, and Baum (2001) argued that the main purposes of a theory are to enable reliable predictions, to synthetize, to give coherence and consistency, and to generalize a large number of observations relating to the same general phenomenon. In this respect, social exchange theory (SET) has recently emerged as a useful framework for understanding individuals' motivations for behaving in an environmentally friendly way in the workplace (Norton, Parker, Zacher, & Ashkanasy, 2015; Yuriev, Boiral, Francoeur, and Paillé, 2018). SET offers all the guarantees listed above.

According to Cropanzano and Mitchell (2005), social exchange theory "is among the most influential conceptual paradigms for understanding workplace behavior" (p. 874). They contend that SET is among the most promising research frameworks for understanding the internal dynamics of organizations. The aim of SET is to determine how social relationships begin, develop, and are maintained over time. Social exchanges have been theorized in a wide range of disciplines, and especially in anthropology, sociology, economics, psychology, management, and, more recently, environmental sustainability. All of these disciplines have examined exchange situations from specific theoretical perspectives by drawing on a range of different methodological approaches and epistemological positions, giving rise to a vast and diverse literature that remains difficult to summarize even now. In fact, it may be more accurate to speak of *theories* rather than *theory*. Given this, since there is no overarching framework for examining social exchanges based on a metatheory, choosing a definition amounts to giving precedence to one discipline over all others. Conscious of these difficulties, I have opted for the definition provided by Blau (1964), according to which social exchanges refer to "the voluntary actions of individuals that are motivated by the returns they are expected to bring and typically do in fact bring from others" (p. 91), a definition rooted in a psychosocial approach of North American inspiration (Ekeh, 1974).

Exchange relationships lie at the heart of human activities. Indeed, they are so deeply rooted in daily habits and routines that we often tend to overlook the general principles that underlie them, give them structure and meaning over the long term, and formalize everyday actions, behaviors and practices. Whether in a social or economic context, an exchange relationship presupposes the existence of several key attributes:

- a good with an intrinsic value at the time of the exchange;
- a market that institutionalizes the circulation of the good between a donor and a recipient;

- a set of obligations binding the donor to the recipient for the duration of the exchange process.

Without realizing it, and regardless of their level of decision-making or their position in the organization chart of the company, employees exchange all kinds of tangible and intangible goods, or at least goods that are identified as such (material benefits, salary, advice, support, know-how, skills, etc.). These goods will have a certain intrinsic value, conferring upon them a greater or lesser degree of interest or importance depending on the situation. For example, a particular skill may be highly valued in one context but have limited value in another. In other words, the context contributes to conferring value to a good. Finally, although the term *value* is generally confined to (or possibly appropriated by) the economic field, it would be wrong to restrict our thinking about exchanged goods in a social exchange context to their sole economic value. A good has both a symbolic and a utilitarian value (Molm, Shaffer, & Collett, 2007).

5.1.1.2   Total Prestations

In its modern form, SET originates from the seminal work of Mauss (1954) in *The Gift*, in which, drawing on his description of traditional societies, Mauss examines the three moral obligations that are giving, receiving, and returning (Frémeaux & Michelson, 2011). As suggested by Gouldner (1960), understanding the motivational bases associated with each of these forms of obligation partly involves viewing egoism and altruism as the two main forms of interest behind the desire of partners to become involved in a social exchange relationship. For social exchange theorists, altruism can be defined, following Batson and Shaw (1991), as "a motivational state with the ultimate goal of increasing another's welfare" (p. 109), while, following Kirchler, Fehr, and Evans (1996), egoism can be examined as a behavioral pattern whereby individuals "strive to maximize their egoistic interests without considering the other's outcome" (p. 315).

The three obligations combine the need to service the moral debt that arises from the gift received, beliefs, and ancient rules of law. On this point, Mauss notes that "*[a]ll these phenomena are at once legal, economic, religious, and even aesthetic and morphological. They are legal, pertaining to both private and public law, organized and diffuse morality, strictly obligatory or simply praised and blamed, at once political and domestic, and involving social classes but also clans and families. They are religious, pertaining to formal religion, magic, animism or to a diffuse religious mentality. They are economic insofar as the ideas of value, utility, interest, luxury, wealth, acquisition and accumulation and, on the other hand, the idea of consumption, and even the idea of pure expenditure, of pure extravagance, are present everywhere, although they carry different meanings to what they mean today"* (p. 274).[1] Mauss came to use the term *total prestation* to denote the idea that exchange institutionalizes relationships between partners.

Mauss went on to note that *"[i]t is not a matter of individuals but of collectivities that are mutually obliged, exchange and enter into contracts: the parties to the contract are legal persons, whether clans, tribes or families, that fight and face each other either in groups by confronting each other on the ground or through their chiefs, or both at the same time. Moreover, the things that they exchange are not exclusively goods or wealth, movable or immovable things – i.e. economically useful things. Above all, they are civilities, feasts, rituals, military ceremonies, women, children, dances, celebrations or festivals in which the market is merely one moment among others and in which the circulation of wealth is just one of the terms of a more general and far more permanent contract. Finally, these prestations and counter-prestations are undertaken in a somewhat voluntary form, through gifts and presents, although they are ultimately strictly obligatory, with war, whether private or public, being the price to pay"* (pp. 150–151).[2] Put differently, in order to understand an exchange, we need to embed it in its context, since that is the only way in which its full meaning can be grasped. An observer choosing to restrict the analysis of partner relationships to a purely mercantile explanation would run the risk of drawing hasty conclusions about individual motivations if they were to ignore the cultural context in which the exchange takes place. In other words, to understand the deep meaning implied by an exchange situation, we need to understand the nature of reciprocity and its moral foundations.

5.1.1.3   Obligations and Reciprocity

In *The Gift*, Mauss presents his major discovery. In his view, reciprocity is a universal mode of regulating exchanges based on the triple obligation

---

[1] Translated from Mauss, M. (2010). *Sociologie et anthropologie*, 12th edition. Paris: PUF.

[2] Translated from Mauss, M. (2010). *Sociologie et anthropologie*, 12th edition. Paris: PUF.

of giving, returning and receiving referred to above. To that extent, social exchange and reciprocity are consubstantial. In a sense, reciprocity constitutes the moral foundations upon which partners base their relationships. In contemporary approaches, reciprocity was first theorized by Gouldner (1960). In his foundational paper "The norm of reciprocity," Gouldner sets out a number of principles guiding the structure of relationships. Reciprocity is a complex process, and adhering to its moral foundations serves to ensure the foundations of lasting relationship. Here, I will focus on just two specific points.

The first point relates to the implicit solidarity pact that serves to embed partners in a lasting exchange relationship. Gouldner reminds us that once it is established as a norm that governs the relationships between individuals, reciprocity requires adherence to the following two principles: (1) people come to the help of those who have helped them in the past and (2) they must not cause harm to those who have helped them previously (p. 171). Though theorized by Gouldner, this idea is not new. It can be found in Chapter 2 of *The Theory of Moral Sentiments* published by Adam Smith In 1759, a decade before *The Wealth of Nations*, where the idea is expressed in the following terms: "*a person should never put himself above another person to the point of hurting him or causing harm to him to accrue a benefit, even if the benefit accrued by the former is far greater than the wrong suffered by the latter*" (pp. 200–201).[3] It can also be found in a paper published by Frédéric Paulhan in 1906 in *Revue Philosophique* in which Paulhan argues that "*Exchange (...) is a very general fact. If we look closely, I believe there is never such a thing as a truly free gift, a unilateral activity. We give and we receive, but the values that the two exchangers give reciprocally are not always analogous*" (p. 366).

The second aspect concerns the distinction between two types of reciprocity: one based on a homeomorphic principle and the other on a heteromorphic principle. Gouldner notes that heteromorphic reciprocity relates to exchanged goods that are different but which are perceived by the partners as having an equivalent estimated value, while homeomorphic reciprocity concerns exchanged goods that are perceived as being strictly comparable in terms of both their form and their value. Homeomorphic reciprocity puts the emphasis on the items exchanged. By contrast, homeomorphic reciprocity emphasizes the circumstances arising from the

---

[3] Translated from Smith A. (1999). *Théorie des sentiments moraux*. Paris: PUF.

exchanged goods. Gouldner suggested that a balance emerges regardless of the form of reciprocity. Exchange relationships thrive in balanced
circumstances but tend to break in the event of an imbalance. However,
the desire to maintain balanced relationships appears theoretically to be
overdetermined and not borne out by subsequent studies. Based on a
review of the relevant literature, Uehara (1995) found that while recipients tend to "repay" the moral debt that they owe to their creditor,
studies suggest that, contrary to a widespread belief, neither creditors
nor beneficiaries seek for a balanced exchange based on homeomorphic
reciprocity.

Gouldner (1960) implicitly acknowledged that, in the vast majority of
cases, it is difficult to identify the starting-point of an exchange between
partners within a system. When social exchange is based on an ideology of
reciprocity shared by several partners, the result over time is an optimal
situation in which the debtor and the creditor are unable to determine
which of the two made the first move (Molm et al., 2007). In the long
term, it thus becomes impossible for one or the other to seek a remedy for
a violated right or compensation for an unfulfilled obligation. However,
although the principle of reciprocity fundamentally underpins the relationships between several partners and appears to be a universal principle,
there remains in SET a significant limitation raised by the following question: who should be the first to initiate action, to make a move? Why?
How? Fundamentally, what these questions raise is the old "chicken-
and-egg" problem. According to Ekeh (1974), while restricted social
exchange is based on a search for the right balance between the rights
and obligations of partners in the short term, generalized social exchange
consists in maintaining long-term interpersonal relationships involving
two partners. We also know, following Molm et al. (2007), that, in the
first case, reciprocity is established on the basis of the utilitarian value
of the good being exchanged, while in the second case reciprocity is
established based on its symbolic value.

Gouldner (1960) goes on to note that, from a utilitarian perspective,
the first move is performed by the party seeking to place the beneficiary in a position of obligation to repay. A sense of debt is thus created,
embedding the beneficiary in a relationship of obligation toward their
donor. Opting for a perspective rooted in an ethics of care, Liedtka
(1996) posited that the onus is on the organization for the following
three reasons. First, it is the responsibility of the company to define the
role of employees within its organizational system. Second, the company

must provide its staff with the necessary resources (e.g., time, means, and development and maintenance of skill levels) to enable them to deliver care to those who need it. Finally, the organization must create the necessary material conditions to establish acts of care (toward people and the environment) as core characteristics of the organizational system. If Liedtka is right, what this implies is that the first move must be made by the employer since the latter is responsible for allocating resources to members of the organization.

5.1.1.4 Social Versus Economic Exchange

Following Mauss, Blau (1964) applied the principles of exchange to modern everyday life.[4] Blau should also be credited for having developed the study of exchange relationships from economic and social perspectives. There is a somewhat contemporary resonance to the terms used to describe the two types of exchange. However, like reciprocity, both forms of exchange also appear to be universal principles.

It would be wrong to assume that forms of economic and social exchange only reflect modern modes of relationship. Indeed, traces of such exchange can be found in various chronicles. I will illustrate the two perspectives by quoting from two excerpts drawn from a story attributed to Àlvero Velho about Vasco de Gama's first expedition to the Indies (1497–1499). The two excerpts are good examples of exchange situations with different implications.

In early January 1498, the crews were short of water and provisions. Vasco de Gama began negotiations with the local lord to secure supplies.

> The captain general sent a navy blazer, red shoes, a hat and a bracelet to the lord. And he told us that if there was anything in his country that we needed, he would happily give it to us. (p. 51)[5]

After a few weeks of sailing along the East African coast, the squadron dropped anchor off an island.

---

[4] However, to do full justice to Mauss's work, it is important to acknowledge that, in the last section of his essay, he sought to apply his findings and observations to the context of the time.

[5] Translated from Vasco de Gama. Le premier Voyage 1497–1499. La relation attribuée à Alvaro Velho. Paris: Edition Chandeine.

In this place and on this island, which they named Monçobiquy, lived a lord, whom they called the sultan, and who was a like a viceroy. He visited our ships many times, accompanied by many of his own people. The captain made sure he ate well and gifted him hats, capes, coral jewelry and many other things. But he was so haughty that he despised everything he was given. He asked for scarlet, but we hadn't brought any, and we gave him what we had. One day, the captain general offered him a light meal, consisting of a large quantity of figs and jams, and he asked him to provide two pilots to accompany us. He answered that he would, subject to being compensated appropriately. So, the captain gave thirty gold coins and two capes to each of them, under the following condition: from the day upon which they received the payment, if they wished to go somewhere, one of the two had to remain on board. They were in perfect agreement in that respect. (p. 58)[6]

At first glance, the two excerpts appear to reflect broadly similar situations. In both cases, an initial action is performed with a view to ensuring the beneficiary settles the debt associated with welcome gifts. However, on closer inspection, we see profound differences between the two situations related, on the one hand, to the implied context and, on the other, to the mutual obligations that they create. The two situations differ radically in terms of their implications. In the first excerpt, the obligation arising from the gifts gives rise, in modern parlance, to a social exchange, since no specification in terms of good or value is anticipated. The debt that arises from the obligation seeks to maintain the bonds of the nascent partnership over the long term. In the second excerpt, the conditions and modes of compensation are, from the outset, clearly set out, leaving little room for relational improvization. The debt arising from the obligation is required to be cleared in the short term.

Both exchange situations have been extensively theorized by contemporary scholars. In broad outline, relationships based on a social exchange feed off the perceived imbalance of the exchanged goods. What matters here is that the imbalance serves to maintain the relationship between partners over the long term. The values of solidarity, altruism and benevolence arising out of the exchange are more important than the exchange itself, which is merely a pretext. The trust between the partners serves to remove the contingent effect of the imbalance from the relationship. As regards economic exchange, the choice of terminology can be misleading.

[6] Idem.

Indeed, while relationships based on economic exchange often require introducing a means of intermediation as a form of currency, they do not always involve tangible goods of a homeomorphic nature. Likewise, such a form of exchange does not necessarily imply absolute parity presupposing equivalent exchanged goods. To a certain extent, economic exchange is similar to bartering, which generally involves a transfer of property and the use of tangible goods. The underlying principle of economic exchange suggests that the obligation binding the partners involved in the exchange arises when the exchanged goods are placed in the market. However, the obligation binding the parties is destined to disappear once the transfer of property has taken place. The principles of equity and justice are called upon when economic exchange is perceived as defective by one of the partners involved in the exchange and an arbitration is required to correct the resulting imbalance.

Blau (1964) highlighted the role of trust in exchange situations in modern societies by basing his claims on previous research on traditional societies. Blau contended that trust is based on past experiences and reflects how reciprocation among partners limits the perception of risk and contributes to nurturing exchanges among them over time. As such, trust can be conceived as a sign of the shared desire of the partners to maintain their social bond. Subsequent empirical work undertaken in various fields of research has sought to put these speculations to the test. For example, Robinson (1996) provided findings indicating that newly hired employees displaying high levels of trust in their employer were less affected by subsequent negative experiences than those who initially reported low levels of trust. Put simply, Robinson demonstrated that loss of trust in the long run is stronger among individuals who view their employers as being untrustworthy. Molm, Takahashi, and Peterson (2000) reported results from an experimental study indicating that, compared with negotiation exchange situations in which taking a risk has limited consequences for individuals, in reciprocation exchange situations the latter are more prone to accept the risk of trusting a partner. In short, their study demonstrates that exchange relationships based on reciprocity involve taking a risk that the partner is trustworthy.

5.1.2   Current Research in an Environmental Sustainability Context

Craddock, Huffman, and Henning (2012) were the first to formally recognize the value of studying environmental sustainability in an organizational context from a social exchange perspective but remained vague about what the theoretical framework of social exchange might contribute to the study of environmental behaviors in a workplace setting. The environmental literature in an organizational context has been providing answers for many years. In particular, the literature has highlighted the effectiveness of behavioral practices which, though not referring to them explicitly, echo the principles developed as part of the social exchange framework. Humphrey, Bord, Hammond, and Mann (1977) showed that encouragement and support from the immediate supervisor over time was conducive to subordinates persisting with manually separating wastepaper in offices. Ramus and Steger (2000) demonstrated that formal support from both the supervisor and the organization contributes to shaping a context conducive to employees engaging in eco-initiatives. Zibarras and Ballinger (2011) reported that informal encouragement by line management was identified in the surveyed organizations as one of the best methods for encouraging staff to behave in an environmentally responsible way at work. Though in different forms, what these early studies have in common is that they emphasize indicators or signals of support by the employer or its representatives as the main lever for driving employee environmental commitment.

The use of social exchange as a theoretical framework provides a means of reconsidering its appearance in the field of environmental sustainability research, offering a basis for a more refined genealogy. While it seems reasonable to suggest that social exchange theory first emerged in the environmental domain as early as the late 1970s, it is only really in the second half of the 2010s that its application to environmental issues has become a constant feature of research in the wider field. While there is a still a long way to go to demonstrate its full heuristic potential, the first applications of social exchange theory to an environmental sustainability context provide results which, though promising, tend, in some cases, to suggest the need to reassess the reasons why employees act responsibly in a work setting.

Based on current research, the environmental literature appears overall to have produced results that are consistent with the standard predictions of social exchange theory. Environmental and GHRM practices are perceived by employees as being important sources of support and encouragement capable of promoting environmental commitment among employees (Paillé, Boiral, & Chen, 2013; Paillé, Valéau, & Renwick, 2020). However, recent findings (Paillé & Meija-Morelos, 2019; Paillé & Valéau, 2020) strongly suggest that the additional environmental efforts made by employees in response to perceived organizational incentives are more the reflection of a form of exchange based on negotiation than a form of exchange founded on reciprocity. What this suggests is that, depending on the circumstances, environmental engagement can be a matter of negotiation between employees and their organization.

5.2   RELATED FIELDS AND OTHER THEORETICAL APPROACHES

The greening of workplaces is neither a concept nor a theory, let alone a new discipline. Rather, it should simply be seen as a particular domain of application: the organizational domain. The greening of workplaces addresses a wide range of issues connected to other related fields. My aim in what follows is not to provide a detailed definition of these related fields, which is something that others have already done in a far better way than I possibly could here. Rather, my more modest aim is to explain in plain terms how the greening of workplaces fits into and develops the knowledge produced in each of these domains.

5.2.1   Sustainability

The term "sustainability" is generally associated with the Brundtland report (1987), in which sustainable development is defined as "development that meets the needs of the present generations without compromising the ability of the future generations to meet their own needs" (p. 43). Here, sustainability is viewed in a broad sense. More specifically, it concerns the three following domains: the social, environmental and economic domains. Sustainability was initially viewed from a global and societal perspective focused on the reduction of poverty through a better distribution of wealth and restrictions on the exploitation of our planet's resources. Subsequently, the field of sustainability has come to be structured around these three main fields, which have, over time, come to develop their own interests and agendas over time (Goodland, 1995). In their editorial for a special issue of *Business, Strategy and the Environment* devoted to the topic of "Trade-offs in corporate sustainability," Hahn, Figge, Pinkse, and Preuss (2010) set out the reasons why it is not, in their view, reasonable to expect organizations to simultaneously fulfill their social, environmental, and economic objectives. While the authors see the possibility of combining all three fields as unrealistic, their contention is that articulating just two of them may, in their view, be a more realistic and adequate option.

The focus of the greening of workplaces as developed in this book is essentially centered around social and environmental forms of sustainability. Social sustainability is defined by Rogers (2014) as "the ability of societies to meet human physical, social, and emotional needs on an ongoing basis" (p. 934). According to Goodland (1995), environmental sustainability "seeks to sustain global life-support system indefinitely (this refers principally to those systems maintaining human life). Source capacities of the global ecosystem provide raw material inputs – food, water, air, energy. Sink capacities assimilate outputs or wastes" (p. 6). Here, organizations have an important role to play in ensuring the greening of workplaces. The articulation of social and environmental sustainability in the workplace reflects the arguments put forward by Vallance, Perkins, and Dixon (2011), who contended that the constraints imposed by human activities on the environment can be limited by allowing the full potential of individuals to express itself. Research on the greening of workplaces offers a range of perspectives that provide avenues for understanding how ecology and the environment fit into the social context of an organization. In that sense, and echoing Chiu (2003), according to whom sustainability provides "the social conditions necessary to support ecological sustainability" (p. 26), the topic of the greening of workplaces explores how social and environmental matters can be articulated by taking organizational challenges and constraints into account.

5.2.2   The Circular Economy

In Geissdoerfer, Savaget, Bocken, and Hultink (2017), the concept of circular economy is defined "as a regenerative system in which resource input and waste, emission, and energy leakage are minimised by slowing, closing, and narrowing material and energy loops. This can be achieved through long-lasting design, maintenance, repair, reuse, remanufacturing, refurbishing, and recycling" (p. 761). In general, the circular economy promotes the analysis of flows conducive to a reduction in resource wastage at the level of a sector of activity (agriculture, construction sector, automobile industry, etc.). In this long process, organizations may be seen as simple operators making use of a wide range of different resources. These resources are metabolized in order to be better valued and sold in a market. Pollution emissions and the production of waste are two collateral effects that are inherent to the process of industrial transformation (or processing). At a global level, the economy as a whole generates 18 times more waste than households, emitting nearly 13 kilograms per capita per day, while households emit an average of less than one kilogram per day per capita (source: Futura, 1 November 2018, Céline Deluzarche).

The circular economy and the greening of workplaces share a similar vision: frugality. They imply considering a range of similar topics, such as recycling, reuse and, in some cases, repairing. To that extent, the two approaches are not dissimilar. However, there is also a difference of scale or level. The circular economy implies operating at a sector or even macroeconomic level. From a circular economy perspective, organizations are viewed as operators within an overall process. By contrast, from a workplace greening point of view, they are treated as black boxes to be opened wide. As argued in this book, the greening of workplaces steers the focus toward the individual level or, as the case may, toward the organizational level, understood as an aggregated form of individual actions.

5.2.3   Stakeholder Theory

Stakeholder theory puts moral principles at the heart of its approach in order to examine the relationships between partners with a greater or lesser interest in the harmonious development of an organization. In his book, Freeman (2010) emphasized that the consideration of stakeholders is not confined to the (simple) notion of cost (p. 59) or to the narrow concept of power (p. 64) but presupposes the integration and sharing of values by organizations and their partners (pp. 96–97). He also noted that the concept of stakeholder may refer to any group, individual or other entity capable of affecting the decisions of an organization. The application of ST to the environmental domain has tended to give rise to in-depth theoretical developments and reflections, although, ultimately, very few empirical studies have been conducted from this perspective. It is now common to examine nature, future generations, and nonhuman species (the biosphere) as stakeholders in their own right, in the same way as investors, employees, customers, governments, service providers, experts (consultants), and pro-environmental interest groups. However, that has not always been the case.

Following the classic definition given by Freeman (2010), a stakeholder is able to shape and direct the actions of other stakeholders through their own actions. To a certain extent, and taking the definition in its strictest sense, we might say that *nature* has the ability to shape the actions of stakeholders in a given organization. The example of the black ice crisis that affected the Province of Québec in the early 1990s shows the extent to which natural events have the potential to paralyze not only human activities as a whole but also economic activities. The more recent example of the COVID-19 crisis has sometimes been construed metaphorically as a warning by Nature (consider, for instance, the opposing positions taken by two former French ministers, Luc Ferry and Nicolas Hulot). The idea is often found in popular culture. A good example of this is *The Happening*, the movie directed by M. Night Shyamalan about Nature's revenge on mankind.

Freeman (2010) argued that environmentalist groups may be viewed as stakeholders. The idea of treating nature or the biosphere as stakeholders also lies at the heart of a debate largely initiated by Starik (1995). The core argument is that nature contributes to business, and renders valuable services to mankind (see WWF, 2018), meaning implicitly that nature as a stakeholder has, in this case, the capacity to contribute to the mainte-nance of relationships through moral attributes such as loyalty, respect, and fairness (Fassin, 2012). Maintaining such a relation assumes at least a willingness to do so. The key question is this: Does Nature have the onto-logical power to behave in this manner? I will leave it to philosophers to answer this question. Suffice to say that the difficulty appears to revolve around the capacity of Nature to reciprocate. Some believe that it is legit-imate to consider that nature has this ability (Starik & Driscoll, 2004). By contrast, others have sought to cast doubt on the capacity of the environ-ment to act as a stakeholder (Phillips & Reichart, 2000). Finally, to fully measure the scale and significance of this question, it is useful to distin-guish between the environment and environmentalists. Environmentalists are human beings. As such, and consistent with Freeman's definition, whether operating as organized groups or as individuals, they have the ability to act and, therefore, to affect a firm's decisions. Finally, if we assume that the natural environment has no ontological reality (simply because it does not think, develops no action strategy, and does not act on the basis of moral principles), the same cannot be said of environmentalist groups, who operate purposefully with the assumed aim of limiting the capacity of organizations to cause environmental harm.

5.2.4   Theory of Planned Behavior (TPB)

The TPB is caught in a paradox. As well as the interest shown by researchers in a wide range of research fields, the unquestionable attractiveness of the theory, evidenced by bibliometric indices (Ajzen, 2011), and its great predictive capacity (Parker, 2011), TPB has also been the target of many criticisms. The point here is not to enter the debate, and even less to contribute to it. Insofar as it leaves no one indifferent, TPB is a living theory, giving rise, in some cases, to heated written debates—which explains its interest at least from an epistemological point of view. Interested readers are referred to several key papers and may decide for themselves about the relative strengths and weaknesses of TPB (e.g., McEachan, Conner, Taylor, & Lawton, 2011; Sniehotta, Presseau, & Araújo-Soares, 2014).

TPB was first developed by Ajzen and Fishbein. The primary aim of TPB is to predict a behavior of interest. Blood donation (Giles, Mcclenahan, Cairns, & Mallet, 2004), entrepreneurial intentions (Van Gelderen et al., 2008), and financial investment behaviors (East, 1993) are just some examples of how the theory has been used and applied. TPB is based on the general principle that a person engages in a particular behavior on a rational basis. An individual's decision to act in a given context is the combined product of individual attitudes, social norms and perceived control. Theoretically, in situations where the attitude and the norm are high, the feeling of control may be low since the personal motivation to act or behave in a particular way will tend to compel the individual to disregard their own perception of the associated constraints (Parker, 2011). In practice, the mounting evidence suggests that, regardless of attitudes and norms, the degree of perceived ease involved in adopting a behavior has a contingent effect on the transition from intention to action, which explains why an increasing number of researchers are restricting the use of TPB to the prediction of intention (Yuriev, Dahmen,

Paillé, Boiral, & Guillaumie, 2020). In that sense, TPB has appeared at times to be shifting toward, or mutating into, a theory of planned *intention*.

TPB is a particularly influential theoretical framework in the environmental literature. In this regard, it is interesting to note that the earliest applications appeared just a few years after the publication of Ajzen's foundational paper. Yuriev et al. (2020) conducted a review of the literature on the use of TPB for predicting pro-environmental behaviors. Several findings emerged from their review. First, between 1995 and 2019, research efforts have tended to focus on environmental behaviors in non-organizational rather than organizational settings. Second, prediction concerns behavioral intention rather than actual behavior—reflecting a partial use of TPB. Apart from a few exceptions (Laudenslager, Holt, & Lofgren, 2004), very few scholars have acknowledged making a partial use only of TPB. This has been a recurring feature of subsequent studies conducted in organizational settings to predict environmental behaviors. Third, the predictive capacity of perceived control has been found to be particularly sensitive to contextual variations—a finding consistent with the following explanations provided by Ajzen (1991): "perceived behavioral control can, and usually does, vary across situations and actions" (p. 184). Fourth, the most widely studied environmental behaviors are recycling or, more precisely, waste sorting, the choice of mode of transport, and energy saving. Lastly, other variables in addition to those usually found in a TPB context have been introduced over the years to improve the prediction of environmental behaviors, such as moral norms, emotions, environmental values, and past behaviors (for a complete list, see Table 3 in Yuriev et al., 2020).

Some concluding remarks

In this chapter, a number of theories and research fields were briefly presented and discussed. Lewin's academic legacy is enormous and has influenced many areas. It is to him that we owe the maxim "There is nothing as practical as a good theory." From this point of view, Lewin clearly understood the value and utility of theories for developing knowledge in the social sciences. All approaches offer well-founded arguments for getting to grips with the greening of workplaces. A decision was made to emphasize social exchange as a theoretical framework—an especially promising framework for the study of environmental issues in an organizational context. Social exchange theory provides a more detailed insight into the reasons why employees voluntarily engage in behaviors that extend beyond the prescribed tasks of their day-to-day work. This point is important since, as I have already noted, environmental behaviors are generally classified in the category of extra-role behaviors. What this means is that an organization cannot formally require its employees to behave in an environmentally responsible way at work. Lastly, unlike other research frameworks, social exchange theory also provides a means of studying environmental behaviors from the point of view of their persistence over time.

REFERENCES

Ajzen, I. (1991). The theory of planned behavior. *Organizational Behavior and Human Decision Processes, 50,* 179–211.

Ajzen, I. (2011). The theory of planned behaviour: Reactions and reflections. *Psychology & Health, 26*(9), 1113–1127.

Batson, C. D., & Shaw, L. L. (1991). Evidence for altruism: Toward a pluralism of prosocial motives. *Psychological Inquiry, 2,* 107–122.

Bell, P. A., Greene, T. C., Fisher, J. D., & Baum, A. (2001). *Environmental psychology* (5th Ed.). London and Belmont, CA: Thomson Wadsworth.

Blau, P. (1964). *Exchange and power in social life.* New York: Wiley.

Chiu, R. (2003). Social sustainability and sustainable housing. In R. Forrest & J. Lee (Eds.), *Housing and social change: East, west perspectives* (pp. 221–239). London, UK: Routledge.

Cordano, M., & Frieze, I. H. (2000). Pollution reduction preferences of US environmental managers: Applying Ajzen's theory of planned behavior. *Academy of Management Journal, 43*(4), 627–641.

Craddock, E. B., Huffman, H. A., & Henning, J. B. (2012). Taming the dragon: How industrial-organizational psychologists can break barriers to "green" business. *Industrial and Organizational Psychology, 5,* 484–487.

Cropanzano, R., & Mitchell, M. S. (2005). Social exchange theory: An interdisciplinary review. *Journal of Management, 31,* 874–900.

Driscoll, C., & Starik, M. (2004). The primordial stakeholder: Advancing the conceptual consideration of stakeholder status for the natural environment. *Journal of Business Ethics, 49*(1), 55–73.

East, R. (1993). Investment decisions and the theory of planned behaviour. *Journal of Economic Psychology, 14*(2), 337–375.

Ekeh, P. (1974). *Social exchange theory. The two traditions.* London: Heinemann.

Fassin, Y. (2012). Stakeholder management, reciprocity and stakeholder responsibility. *Journal of Business Ethics, 109*(1), 83–96.

Freeman, R. E. (2010). *Strategic management: A stakeholder approach.* Cambridge: Cambridge University Press.

Frémeaux, S., & Michelson, G. (2011). 'No strings attached': Welcoming the existential gift in business. *Journal of Business Ethics, 99*(1), 63–75.

Geissdoerfer, M., Savaget, P., Bocken, N. M., & Hultink, E. J. (2017). The circular economy–A new sustainability paradigm? *Journal of Cleaner Production, 143,* 757–768.

Giles, M., Mcclenahan, C., Cairns, E., & Mallet, J. (2004). An application of the theory of planned behaviour to blood donation: The importance of self-efficacy. *Health Education Research, 19*(4), 380–391.

Goodland, R. (1995). The concept of environmental sustainability. *Annual Review of Ecology and Systematics, 26*(1), 1–24.

Gouldner, A. W. (1960). The norm of reciprocity: A preliminary statement. *American Sociological Review, 25,* 161–178.

Hahn, T., Figge, F., Pinkse, J., & Preuss, L. (2010). Trade-offs in corporate sustainability: You can't have your cake and eat it. *Business Strategy and the Environment, 19*(4), 217–229.

Humphrey, C. R., Bord, R. J., Hammond, M. M., & Mann, S. H. (1977). Attitudes and conditions for cooperation in a paper recycling program. *Environment and Behavior, 9,* 107–124.

Kirchler, E., Fehr, E., & Evans, R. (1996). Social exchange in the labor market: Reciprocity and trust versus egoistic money maximization. *Journal of Economic Psychology, 17*(3), 313–341.

Laudenslager, M. S., Holt, D. T., & Lofgren, S. T. (2004). Understanding air force members' intentions to participate in pro-environmental behaviors: An application of the theory of planned behavior. *Perceptual and Motor Skills, 98*(3), 1162–1170.

Liedtka, J. M. (1996). Feminist morality and competitive reality: A role for an ethic of care? *Business Ethics Quarterly, 6*(2), 179–200.

Mauss, M. (1954). *The gift.* London: Cohen & West.

McEachan, R. R. C., Conner, M., Taylor, N., & Lawton, R. J. (2011). Prospective prediction of health-related behaviors with the theory of planned behavior: A meta-analysis. *Health Psychology Review, 5,* 97–144.

Molm, L. D., Schaefer, D. R., & Collett, J. L. (2007). The value of reciprocity. *Social Psychology Quarterly, 70*(2), 199–217.

Molm, L. D., Takahashi, N., & Peterson, G. (2000). Risk and trust in social exchange: An experimental test of a classical proposition. *American Journal of Sociology, 105*(5), 1396–1427.

Norton, T. A., Parker, S. L., Zacher, H., & Ashkanasy, N. M. (2015). Employee green behavior: A theoretical framework, multilevel review, and future research agenda. *Organization & Environment, 28*(1), 103–125.

Paillé, P., Boiral, O., & Chen, Y. (2013). Linking environmental management practices and organizational citizenship behaviour for the environment: A social exchange perspective. *International Journal of Human Resource Management, 24,* 3552–3575.

Paillé, P., & Meija-Morelos, J. H. (2019). Organisational support is not always enough to encourage employee environmental performance. The moderating role of exchange ideology. *Journal of Cleaner Production, 220,* 1061–1070.

Paillé, P., & Valéau, P. (2020). "I don't owe you, but I Am committed": Does felt obligation matter on the effect of green training on employee environmental commitment? *Organization & Environment,* 1086026620921453.

Paillé, P., Valéau, P., & Renwick, D. W. (2020). Leveraging green human resource practices to achieve environmental sustainability. *Journal of Cleaner Production,* 121137.

Parker, R. (2011). Green organisational performance: Behavioural change interventions based on the theory of planned behaviour. In *Going green: The psychology of sustainability in the workplace* (pp. 36–46). Leicester: The British Psychological Society.

Paulhan, F. (1906, Juillet-Décembre). L'échange économique et l'échange affectif: le sentiment dans la vie sociale. *Revue philosophique,* 359–399.

Phillips, R. A., & Reichart, J. (2000). The environment as a stakeholder? A fairness-based approach. *Journal of Business Ethics, 23*(2), 185–197.

Ramus, C., & Steger, U. (2000). The roles of supervisory support behaviors and environmental policy in employee eco-initiatives at leading-edge European companies. *Academy of Management Journal, 43,* 605–626.

Robinson, S. L. (1996). Trust and breach of the psychological contract. *Administrative Science Quarterly, 41*(4).

Rogers, D. S. (2014). Socioeconomic equity and sustainability. *Global Environmental Change, 1,* 933–941.

Smith, A. (1999).*Théorie des sentiments moraux.* Paris: PUF.

Sniehotta, F. F., Presseau, J., & Araújo-Soares, V. (2014, January). Time to retire the theory of planned behaviour. *Health Psychology Review, 8*(1), 1–7.

Starik, M. (1995). Should trees have managerial standing? Toward stakeholder status for non-human nature. *Journal of Business Ethics, 14*(3), 207–217.

Steg, L., & Vlek, C. (2009). Encouraging pro-environmental behaviour: An integrative review and research agenda. *Journal of Environmental Psychology, 29*(3), 309–317.

Uehara, E. S. (1995). Reciprocity reconsidered: Gouldner's moral norm of reciprocity and social support. *Journal of Social and Personal Relationships, 12*(4), 483–502.

Vallance, S., Perkins, H. C., & Dixon, J. E. (2011). What is social sustainability? A clarification of concepts. *Geoforum, 42*(3), 342–348.

Van Gelderen, M., Brand, M., van Praag, M., Bodewes, W., Poutsma, E., & Van Gils, A. (2008). Explaining entrepreneurial intentions by means of the theory of planned behaviour. *Career Development International, 13*(6), 538–559.

World Commission on Environment and Development, & Brundtland, G. H. (1987). *Presentation of the Report of the World Commission on Environment and Development to the Commission of the European Communities, the EC and EFTA Countries... 5 May 1987, Brussels.* World Commission on Environment and Development.

WWF. (2018). *Living planet report 2018: Aiming higher* (Eds. N. Grooten & R. E. A. Almond). Gland, Switzerland: WWF.

Yuriev, A., Boiral, O., Francoeur, V., & Paillé, P. (2018). Overcoming the barriers to pro-environmental behaviors in the workplace: A systematic review. *Journal of Cleaner Production, 182,* 379–394.

Yuriev, A., Dahmen, M., Paillé, P., Boiral, O., & Guillaumie, L. (2020). Pro-environmental behaviors through the lens of the theory of planned behavior: A scoping review. *Resources, Conservation and Recycling, 155,* 104660.

Zibarras, L., & Ballinger, C. (2011). Promoting environmental behaviour in the workplace: A survey of UK organisations. In *Going green: The psychology of sustainability in the workplace* (pp. 84–90). Leicester: British Psychological Society.

CHAPTER 6

The Question of Organizational Boundaries

Abstract Many studies have reported that individuals behave differently toward the environment depending on the context in which they find themselves. This chapter aims to describe "the border model" (as developed by Clark, *Human Relations* 53: 747–770, 2000) and to apply the model to the greening of workplaces with a view to examining the principles for understanding how organizational and non-organizational settings exert different pressures on individuals. The chapter also discusses the few studies that have sought to explain how organizations looking to reduce their environmental impact are able to take advantage of the individual habits and skills developed by their employees outside the boundaries of their organization.

Keywords Environmental domains · Organizational boundaries · Border theory

6.1 PRO-ENVIRONMENTAL BEHAVIORS: WITHIN AND OUTSIDE THE WORKPLACE

6.1.1 Similarities and Differences

A comparison of studies conducted on environmental behaviors in work and nonwork settings reveals a striking convergence. Overall, and leaving

© The Author(s) 2020   77
P. Paillé, *Greening the Workplace*,
https://doi.org/10.1007/978-3-030-58388-0_6

aside minor nuances, the environmental behaviors examined in both settings have tended to be broadly the same. Roughly the same questions have tended to be addressed, and these generally revolve around definitions, driving factors, and intervention methods aimed at changing habits and routines.

One question raised by this apparent similarity is whether different spheres within and outside the work environment represent domains or categories involving artificial distinctions. At a micro level—i.e., at the subjective employee level—the fields within and outside work appear to generate their own specific constraints. The same individual may sometimes be faced with a whole range of constraints and pressures impacting their ability to behave consistently from one environment to another. The following pages aim to illustrate the degree of similarity between these two research streams.

6.1.1.1   Pro-Environmental Behaviors in a Private Setting

Behaviors in this context have been the subject of a number of studies in the area of environmental sociology and psychology (see, for example, Gosling & Williams, 2010; Stern, 2000) and take many different forms. According to the typology developed by Stern (2000), environmentally significant behaviors can involve environmental activism (e.g., involvement in nongovernmental organizations, petitioning, and demonstrations), non-activist behaviors in the public sphere (e.g., support for environmental policies and regulations), private-sphere environmentalism (e.g., green purchasing practices, recycling, reduction of water consumption), and other environmental behaviors (including within organizations). Private-sphere environmentalism is the most common and most widely studied type of environmental behavior outside the workplace. The motivations behind these behaviors have been associated with a wide variety of factors, including, among others, the perceived costs and benefits, personal knowledge, value systems, the locus of control, normative beliefs, attitudes toward behavior, and green identity (e.g., Whitmarsh & O'Neill, 2010). Finally, research has also been conducted on the effectiveness and implications of private eco-initiatives. Overall, although the benefits of these initiatives may be small when considered in isolation, their aggregated effects and global contribution to environmental sustainability have been shown to be significant (see, for example, Tukker, Cohen, Hubacek, & Mont, 2010).

6.1.1.2   Pro-Environmental Behaviors in an Organizational Setting

Except for a small number of prior studies (Lee, De Young, & Marrans, 1995), this stream of research is a recent development. Interestingly, while pro-environmental actions in the private sphere have typically been viewed as discretionary (see Steg & Vlek, 2009), depending on the nature of the job and the type of industry, the evidence indicates that PEBs in the workplace are also performed on a discretionary basis (Norton, Parker, Zacher, & Ashkanasy, 2015; Ones & Dilchert, 2012). In the same way as environmental behaviors in the private sphere, PEBs can take very different forms. As discussed in Chapter 2, employees may behave in an eco-friendly manner by avoiding harm (including by preventing pollution, monitoring environmental impacts, and strengthening ecosystems), conserving resources (e.g., limiting waste, reducing use, reusing, and recycling), working sustainably (e.g., changing work habits, embracing innovation for sustainability, and creating sustainable processes), influencing others (e.g., encouraging and educating), taking initiatives (e.g., lobbying and activism), helping teammates to implement green procedures, and sharing environmental values with organizational members.

6.1.1.3   Behavioral Continuity Versus Behavioral Discontinuity

The similarity of environmental behaviors in the private and professional spheres suggests the possibility of a behavioral continuum. In a sense, it seems reasonable to assume that making efforts to reduce electricity consumption at home (where motivation involves environmental concerns rather than being driven by purely economic considerations) is not significantly different from seeking to limit the consumption of electricity at work. Finally, with this type of behavior, the habits acquired by an individual in one of the two spheres do not require different habits when applied by the same individual in the other sphere. The facts of the matter are likely to be significantly different in the case of environmental behaviors that depend on specific arrangements being put in place. For example, recycling habits developed in the private sphere can be difficult to transfer to the professional sphere if appropriate arrangements are not made within the work environment. In this case, the physical conditions of the context are the key factors that generate the conditions of discontinuity and that complicate the process of transferring habits from one context to another difficult.

In their everyday life, individuals tend to operate in several different spheres, including domestic, professional and social spheres. One important question addressed by recent environmental research is the question of behavioral persistence when individuals move from one sphere to another. For example, to what extent is an individual accustomed to recycling at home free to extend the same habit by applying it in other spheres, such as the work sphere? Similarly, can an individual largely unconcerned about environmental matters in their private sphere be encouraged to adopt pro-environmental behaviors through incentives when changing spheres? To put it differently, the aim is to understand whether changing sphere leads to a change in intentions toward the environment and, therefore, to a change in behavior.

In order to properly address the question of behavioral plasticity toward the environment, we need to consider the factors that inhibit or facilitate the transfer of environmental habits from one sphere to another. Chief among these factors is the principle of the separation of spheres embodied by the notion of border. The principle of the separation of life spheres is the subject of a vast literature across many disciplines. However, although the question of separation continues to be largely ignored in research on environmental behaviors, a number of studies offer a new way of thinking about environmental behaviors as a whole.

6.1.2   Organizational Boundaries and the Limits of Behavioral Persistence

6.1.2.1   Issue

Ramus and Killmer (2007) introduced the idea that organizational boundaries play an important but neglected role in the intention of individuals to behave pro-environmentally (or not, as the case may). In that sense, organizational boundaries represent an increasingly important aspect of people's lives, shaping their general behavior toward the environment.

We might assume that boundaries have a different influence depending on whether or not employees hold a managerial position. For example, it has been suggested that, compared to their subordinates, managers have more leeway in terms of their ability to behave in an environmentally responsible manner at work (Ones & Dilchert, 2012). Put differently, managers have, by nature, the necessary and sufficient autonomy to behave in an environmentally responsible way in all circumstances.

Equally, their subordinates do not have the necessary leeway to behave in an environmentally friendly way as independent agents. In other words, the strong implication is that while some individuals act without needing to be stimulated or driven to do so, others (i.e., subordinates) need encouragement. In my view, although this position overstates the capacity of employees in a job endowed with the attributes of hierarchy to act and behave freely, it also underestimates the ability of employees who do not have these attributes to engage in environmentally friendly behaviors in their day-to-day work. The recent literature on the subject has tended to question the assumed freedom of managers in their behavior toward the environment and to reassess the assumed contingent effect of the lack of leeway (or scope for action) on nonmanagerial employees.

6.1.2.2   Evidence
An individual's position within the organizational hierarchy is no guarantee that they will be not be affected by organizational contingencies. Research shows that managerial employees can have conflicting experiences. For example, having examined a group of managers from four different companies in the automobile industry, Fineman (1997) found that those who practiced recycling in their private sphere and who sought to instill these habits in their children struggled to apply the same habits in the workplace. By contrast, based on a sample of managers working for multinationals, Velsor and Quinn (2012) demonstrated the existence of a principle of transposition of environmental habits from the private sphere to the work sphere, strongly indicating an ability to transfer environmental practices from one sphere to another among the managers observed. Other studies devoted to nonmanagerial employees have yielded comparable behavioral models. For example, by observing a group of office workers, Lee et al. (1995) found that those who recycled the most at home were also those who recycled the most at work. By contrast, Wells, Taheri, Gregory-Smith, and Manika (2016) found that employees accustomed to adopting energy-saving practices in order to limit energy use for reasons other than financial considerations tended not to transfer the same habits to the workplace.

6.2   Border Theory

6.2.1   Premises

Border theory is a research framework used in a wide range of disciplines (Brunet-Jailly, 2005), but has remained somewhat neglected in the environmental field, despite the fact that the question of borders is implicitly addressed in studies that have examined the persistence of environmental behaviors when individuals move from one sphere to another—for example, from the private to the professional sphere.

Clark (2000) developed her border theory as a means of remedying the vagueness of the conceptual frameworks used in research to describe the interactions between individuals' domestic and professional spheres when moving from one sphere to another. According to Clark, spillover and compensation theories are inadequate in several respects. Clark argues that, in their initial version, both theories suffered mainly from being too dependent on their respective premises and, above all, from viewing the individual as a prisoner of their own psychological state when leaving one sphere for another. In doing so, they ignore the real-world situations in which individuals are able to compromise with their own desires and to reach solutions that are nonetheless consistent with their desires, thereby achieving their behavioral intentions. For example, individuals with a personality dominated by a negative emotion in one sphere tend to maintain that state when changing sphere. According to compensation theory, individuals frustrated in one sphere are able to find sources of personal fulfillment when changing sphere.

According to Clark (2000), later conceptual additions failed to provide decisive solutions for the imperfections found in spillover and compensation theories, primarily because, in her view, a description had yet to be provided to fully understand, on the one hand, why the interaction between two different spheres potentially leads to conflicts and, on the other, how a balance between the two spheres is achieved. Therefore, Clark suggests that we need to address these deficiencies by developing a border theory designed to explain how and why individuals are able to achieve a balance when moving from one sphere to another.

6.2.2   Key Concepts

Border theory is structured around the following four concepts: the domain of activity, boundaries, and border crossers and keepers.

6.2.2.1   Domain (From Home to Work)

The first concept is the notion of domain (or sphere) of activity. Unlike the three other concepts, Clark does not provide a clear definition of what she means by the term "domain." She proposes nonetheless to start from shared values and to emphasize culture by way of establishing a difference between the different domains—which amounts to saying that domains are defined less by their substance than by what distinguishes them from other domains. For reasons of concision, the domains considered here and in the following pages will be limited to the private and professional spheres. Muster and Schrader (2011) posited that when individuals have eco-friendly habits in the nonwork domain, they tend to develop transferable skills that can be more or less easily mobilized in the work domain. For example, initiatives involving paper recycling, reducing water consumption or improving energy efficiency (e.g., turning off lights and turning down heating before leaving a room) are generally based on similar attitudes, regardless of the context. Manika, Wells, Gregory-Smith, and Gentry (2015) recently provided findings that support this possibility. In short, it can be assumed that the development of environmental habits in one's private life positively influences engagement in environmental sustainability in a work context.

6.2.2.2   Boundaries

Boundaries are "lines of demarcation between domains, defining the point at which domain-relevant behavior begins and ends" (p. 756). According to Clark, the domestic and professional spheres are separated by three types of boundaries: physical, temporal, and psychological. The physical boundary is probably the easiest to represent (for both the employee and the observer). Crossing the threshold of the organization unambiguously means that the employee has entered or exited the work domain at the beginning or end of the working day. The temporal boundary corresponds to the amount of time spent engaging in the main activity of the domain—in other words, the number of hours spent carrying out work in the professional domain or the amount of time devoted to family activities in the domestic domain. Finally, the psychological boundary establishes all the individual behaviors to be adopted in order to adhere to the rules governing life in a given domain. I propose to complete this picture by adding a moral boundary designed to define the axiological framework governing adherence to individual principles. In that sense, a personal sense or feeling of moral transgression may signify the crossing of a boundary between doing what is right and committing morally reprehensible acts. Clark (2000) also notes that the different boundaries have the peculiarity of overlapping to a greater or lesser extent depending on the circumstances. We are required to cross the various boundaries on a regular basis for brief periods of time, with each boundary having to be crossed several times over the course of the same day.

6.2.2.3   Border Crossers and Border Keepers

Border crossers and border keepers are able to exert influence. Because of this, they are an important source of identification for individuals who cross the boundaries between several domains on a regular basis. Clark indicates that border crossers behave differently according to the attributes listed in Fig. 6.1. The degree of influence combined with the level of identification determine the individual's ability to manage the constraints of boundaries and to act as an agent of change. The higher the level of influence and identification, the easier it is to move from one domain to another; conversely, the lower the level of influence and identification, the harder it is to move between domains.

6.2.3   Findings

To date, only a limited amount of research has been conducted on environmental behaviors from the point of view of boundaries. While it offers a useful heuristic basis, the model developed by Clark (2000) has rarely been tested in an environmental context. Though not explicitly drawing on this model as a theoretical reference framework, a small number of

Central	Peripheral
→ Internalized the domain's culture and values	→ Ignorance of, or disdain for, the values or cultural norms of the domain
→ Demonstrated competence in one's responsibilities	
→ Connected with others who have central membership	→ Full competence not yet achieved
→ Identified personally with domain responsibilities	→ Lack of interaction with other members
	→ Little or no sense of responsibility for the domain
Strong influence and identification	Weak influence and identification

Fig. 6.1   Main attributes of border crossers (Based on Clark, 2000)

studies provide a good indication of the usefulness of examining the role of boundaries for understanding how employees behave toward the environment. Here, three studies will be discussed by applying the notion of boundary from a different angle. The first study points to a psychological boundary that causes employees to reduce their scope of action. The second study envisages boundaries by examining the passage from one domain to another in terms of behavioral persistence. Finally, the third study examines boundaries as a metaphor for understanding how less environmentally active employees can be encouraged to become more environmentally responsible.

6.2.3.1   Study 1
In the case of Cordano and Hanson Frieze (2000), these limits appear to be of a psychological nature since one of their findings was that, based on their past experience acquired in other organizations, environmental managers appear to be confident about their ability to put in place measures aimed at reducing pollution sources within their organization. The authors explained that they had to adapt their methodological approach to take into account the fact that, in spite of their role and hierarchical position, the participants reported having a limited capacity to bring about change in their organization's environmental policies. As a result, the authors were forced to adapt the section of their questionnaire relating to "Behavioral preference for source reduction activity" by amending it to "I would like to......" (instead of "I intend to ...."). The amendment is a telling detail that says much about the existence of limits in organizations.

6.2.3.2   Study 2
Chen, Chen, Huang, Long, and Li (2017) examined behavioral consistency by comparing environmental engagement in three domains: the private, public, and professional domains. Four types of environmental behaviors were considered: basic behaviors (corresponding to direct behaviors), decision-making (corresponding to the degree or extent to which an individual perceives that their actions are effective), interpersonal behaviors (corresponding to indirect environmental behaviors in the form of encouragement and education), and civic environmental behavior (corresponding to the category "personal development"). Their study yielded the following results. When considered as a whole, environmental behaviors occur to a greater extent in the work and private domains and

to a comparatively lesser extent in the public domain. When examined individually, and focusing solely on the private and professional domains, the results indicate, on the one hand, that basic and civic environmental behaviors are exhibited in the professional domain to a greater extent that in the private domain and, on the other hand, that decision-making and interpersonal behavior occur more frequently in the professional domain than in the private domain. Among other findings, the study by Chen et al. (2017) shows overall that individual forms of pro-environmental engagement vary according to context and that these differences are explained by the intrinsic characteristics of each context. The professional and private domains are known to be more responsive to the effects of individual actions since they allow for a limited number of people to be mobilized around the environmental cause. The public domain requires collective mobilization, which may be perceived as time-intensive at the individual level.

Although Chen et al. did not discuss their results by resorting explicitly to the concept of boundary, by extrapolation it seems possible, on the basis of their study, to clarify how individuals manage their environmental contribution depending on the domains in which they operate. Thus, if we apply Clark's arguments to the study by Chen et al., the implication is that in crossing boundaries (home → work and work → home), an individual will occupy a central or peripheral position depending on both the context and the behavior. The individual's position will depend on their ability to act with perseverance (i.e., consistently) by basing their current actions on their past environmental behaviors. An individual will be considered central if they demonstrate behavioral persistence by crossing the boundaries separating one context from another. Their ability to demonstrate environmental leadership in relation to their colleagues is dependent on their ability to assume their environmental responsibilities by sharing their environmental skills and knowledge. On the other hand, an individual will be deemed peripheral if they are unable to demonstrate behavioral persistence when moving from one domain to another. Accordingly, the effect of their environmental leadership on other members of the organization will be limited because of the limited scope for sharing their skills.

6.2.3.3   Study 3

In the model developed by Clark (2000), the immediate supervisor plays an important role by acting as a facilitator for the transition from the nonwork domain to the work domain. Research on environmental matters in a work context has acknowledged the importance of the role of the immediate supervisor acting as a provider of emotional and instrumental resources that enable employees to behave in environmentally responsible ways (for a recent overview, see Robertson and Barling). Drawing on the premises of border theory, Paillé, Raineri, and Boiral (2019) showed that the immediate supervisor can also facilitate the crossing of mental boundaries (for more details, see Ashforth, Kreiner, & Fugate, 2000). Paillé et al. (2019) demonstrated the existence of four behavioral profiles toward the environment. The four profiles are obtained by comparing the low and high levels of environmental behavioral engagement exhibited within and outside work. Employees may be Enthusiasts (high in both private and work domains), Conformists (low in private domain and high in work domain), Citizens (high in private domain and low in work domain) or Apathetics (low in both private and work domains).

The aim of Paillé et al. was to identify the driving factors that enable an employee to move from one profile to another—i.e., the factors that cause employees with little interest in environmental matters to behave as employees with a deep concern for the environment. Five drivers were mobilized. Two are of an organizational nature (i.e., environmental management practices and the environmental support provided by the immediate supervisor), while three are of a psychological nature (i.e., commitment to the organization, self-efficacy, and personal environmental beliefs). The results obtained "reveal that supervisory support plays an important role when coupled with affective commitment, especially for individuals displaying a low level of environmental concern both at work and at home (i.e. Apathetics) compared to those who are only environmentally committed at home (i.e. Citizens)" (p. 263). The study shows that while the environmental support provided by the immediate supervisor may be said to be a decisive factor since it enables employees with a particularly low level of interest in environmental matters to behave in an environmentally responsible way, it cannot fully play its part without some sense (however minimal) of personal affiliation with the organization (engagement). In other words, what this suggests is that environmentally unconcerned employees also respond favorably to the environmental support provided by their immediate supervisor for reasons of organizational conformity.

Some concluding remarks

Organizations with an interest in greening their workplace should be able to derive a great many benefits from the environmental skills, knowledge, and habits acquired by their employees in spheres other than the work domain. In other words, the responsibility of an organization is to recognize, assess, and appreciate the full value of its employees' environmental knowledge. Put differently, organizations have much to learn about environmental matters from their members. Yet individuals face more or less tangible borders on a daily basis. These borders create powerful constraints on individual action and, in doing so, significantly influence the tendency of individuals to persist in behaving favorably toward the environment. The studies discussed in this chapter indicate that the constraints imposed by organizational limits affect all employees, whether or not they work in a managerial position. The evidence shows that behavioral persistence does not depend on the individual's role within the organization or on their position within the organizational hierarchy. The next chapter will aim to offer an explanation for this fact by examining the different obstacles faced by employees in their work environments.

REFERENCES

Ashforth, B. E., Kreiner, G. E., & Fugate, M. (2000). All in a day's work: Boundaries and micro role transitions. *Academy of Management Review, 25*(3), 472–491.

Brunet-Jailly, E. (2005). Theorizing borders: An interdisciplinary perspective. *Geopolitics, 10*(4), 633–649.

Chen, H., Chen, F., Huang, X., Long, R., & Li, W. (2017). Are individuals' environmental behavior always consistent? An analysis based on spatial difference. *Resources, Conservation and Recycling, 125,* 25–36.

Clark, S. C. (2000). Work/family border theory: A new theory of work/family balance. *Human Relations, 53*(6), 747–770.

Cordano, M., & Frieze, I. H. (2000). Pollution reduction preferences of US environmental managers: Applying Ajzen's theory of planned behavior. *Academy of Management Journal, 43*(4), 627–641.

Fineman, S. (1997). Constructing the green manager. *British Journal of Management, 8*(1), 31–38.

Gosling, E., & Williams, K. J. (2010). Connectedness to nature, place attachment and conservation behaviour: Testing connectedness theory among farmers. *Journal of Environmental Psychology, 30*(3), 298–304.

Lee, Y. J., De Young, R., & Marans, R. W. (1995). Factors influencing individual recycling behavior in office settings: A study of office workers in Taiwan. *Environment and Behavior, 27*(3), 380–403.

Manika, D., Wells, V. K., Gregory-Smith, D., & Gentry, M. (2015). The impact of individual attitudinal and organisational variables on workplace environmentally friendly behaviours. *Journal of Business Ethics, 126*(4), 663–684.

Muster, V., & Schrader, U. (2011). Green work-life balance: A new perspective for green HRM. *German Journal of Human Resource Management, 25*(2), 140–156.

Norton, T. A., Parker, S. L., Zacher, H., & Ashkanasy, N. M. (2015). Employee green behavior: A theoretical framework, multilevel review, and future research agenda. *Organization & Environment, 28*(1), 103–125.

Ones, D. S., & Dilchert, S. (2012). Environmental sustainability at work: A call to action. *Industrial and Organizational Psychology, 5*(4), 444–466.

Paillé, P., Raineri, N., & Boiral, O. (2019). Environmental behavior on and off the job: A configurational approach. *Journal of Business Ethics, 158*(1), 253–268.

Ramus, C. A., & Killmer, A. B. (2007). Corporate greening through prosocial extrarole behaviours—A conceptual framework for employee motivation. *Business Strategy and the Environment, 16*(8), 554–570.

Steg, L., & Vlek, C. (2009). Encouraging pro-environmental behaviour: An integrative review and research agenda. *Journal of Environmental Psychology, 29*(3), 309–317.

Stern, P. C. (2000). New environmental theories: Toward a coherent theory of environmentally significant behavior. *Journal of Social Issues, 56*(3), 407–424.

Tukker, A., Cohen, M. J., Hubacek, K., & Mont, O. (2010). The impacts of household consumption and options for change. *Journal of Industrial Ecology, 14*(1), 13–30.

Van Velsor, E., & Quinn, L. (2012). Leadership and environmental sustainability. In S. E. Jackson, D. S. Ones, & S. Dilchert (Eds.), *Managing human resources for environmental sustainability* (Vol. 32, pp. 241–261). Wiley.

Wells, V. K., Taheri, B., Gregory-Smith, D., & Manika, D. (2016). The role of generativity and attitudes on employees home and workplace water and energy saving behaviours. *Tourism Management, 56*, 63–74.

Whitmarsh, L., & O'Neill, S. (2010). Green identity, green living? The role of pro-environmental self-identity in determining consistency across diverse pro-environmental behaviours. *Journal of Environmental Psychology, 30*(3), 305–314.

CHAPTER 7

Employees and Pro-Environmental Behaviors: Obstacles, Constraints, and Barriers

Abstract This chapter provides an original analysis of barriers to the adoption of pro-environmental behaviors by individuals. An overview of the literature on environmental issues shows that the study of obstacles to environmental engagement at the individual level has attracted limited attention compared to research on incentives and facilitators. This chapter provides an overview of the current state of knowledge on factors that limit the likelihood of employees adopting pro-environmental behaviors in the workplace. The chapter draws on Lewinian field theory as an analytical framework and examines the extent to which, depending on their degree of physical and mental proximity (whether real or perceived), employees feel hindered in their environmental engagement.

Keywords Obstacles · Levels · Lewinian field · Mental representation

7.1 Obstacles in the Workplace: A Brief Commentary on the Current State of Knowledge

An overview of the specialized literature on environmental behaviors might lead one to conclude that the study of obstacles is a relatively minor area of research in comparison to the number of studies devoted to incentives and facilitators. However, there have been a number of attempts over the years to rank and categorize obstacles. For the most part, these

© The Author(s) 2020
P. Paillé, *Greening the Workplace*,
https://Doi.org/10.1007/978-3-030-58388-0_7

have tended to focus on the study of obstacles, or barriers, to environmental commitment and engagement in nonwork settings (Gifford, 2011;
Kollmuss & Agyeman, 2002; Lorenzoni, Nicholson-Cole, & Whitmarsh,
2007). Though not neglected, research on obstacles in a work context
suffers from a lack of visibility that, in my view, can be explained by a lack
of structure around the knowledge developed in this area rather than any
real lack of interest in the question itself.

Individuals face a range of obstacles in the workplace. These can
be grouped into four categories or levels: institutional, organizational,
managerial, and individual (i.e., psychological). These four categories also
provide a means of understanding the different reasons people give in
order to justify their lack of environmental engagement.

7.1.1   Institutional Level

Institutional obstacles include normative constraints that are external to
the organization and that govern, structure, and regulate the internal
conduct of operational processes. The legislative framework creates obstacles related to the availability and clarity of information, the perceived ease
of its applicability, and the flexibility of organizational characteristics and
specificities (Jabbour et al., 2016). The management system relating to
environmental standards can also give rise to obstacles if senior management is uncertain about the anticipated effects or results, if it believes that
the costs and complexity associated with introducing standards outweigh
the benefits of holding certifications, and if it believes that being certi-
fied might affect the competitiveness of the organization (Jabbour et al.,
2016).

7.1.2   Organizational Level

Obstacles at the organizational level typically involve strategic and financial considerations and may refer to the costs associated with launching
and maintaining sustainability initiatives, a lack of relevant resources in
terms of capacity and knowledge, limited financial capacity for environmental investments, difficulties in measuring return on investment, and
lack of support from senior management (Jabbour et al. 2016).

In a primarily descriptive study, Schmit, Fegley, Esen, Schramm,
and Tomassetti (2012) interviewed 728 individuals in human resource
management roles with a view to answering a number of questions aimed

at better understanding the role of the HR function in implementing an organizational policy for sustainable development. Their findings indicate that organizations resort to a whole range of obstacles designed to hamper efforts to put in place an organizational policy for the purpose of promoting the environment. The reasons invoked relate to the perception of the internal barriers identified by the respondents (369 out of 748) as being difficult to overcome within their organization. The reasons identified by the study point to relatively different justifications in terms of content. Several of them are clearly justifications of an accounting and financial nature, such as implementation costs (38%), the difficulty of measuring return on investment (35%), and the cost of maintaining facilities and installations (31%). Others relate to justifications of a strategic nature, such as lack of support for environmental matters from senior management (34%), the incompatibility between environmental considerations and the organization's primary objectives (21%), a perceived lack of competitive advantage (18%), and low shareholder support (5%).

7.1.3   Managerial Level

Obstacles at the managerial level hamper the action of managers differently according to the latter's position within the organizational hierarchy, but also according to their capacity to exert influence in management meetings so as to get their point across in drawing attention to the environmental question. A senior manager will probably have a greater capacity to exert influence than a line manager. Leadership in the context of environmental sustainability has attracted considerable attention in this respect (Robertson & Barling, 2015). Most research in this area has focused on environmental leadership, which, according to Egri and Herman (2000), refers to "the ability to influence individuals and mobilize organisations to realise a vision of long-term ecological sustainability" (p. 572). Through their capacity to influence, senior managers can encourage an environmental vision and are able to determine the allocation of the financial, technical, and human resources necessary for its implementation. Conversely, they may choose to relegate environmental issues as a matter of secondary concern or neglect them altogether by focusing their efforts on other organizational issues.

Zibarras and Ballinger (2011) conducted a survey among 147 human resource professionals in Britain working for public and private organizations. Their survey revealed that respondents believe the barriers hindering their organization's commitment to environmental issues are explained in 65% of cases by unclear environmental leadership, strategies, and goals and in 57% of cases by the organization prioritizing commercial objectives above environmental considerations. In other words, a manager may have an interest in environmental matters but be limited in practice by their position within the organizational hierarchy (Cordano & Frieze, 2000), but also by the fact of having no outlet by virtue of not being a member of a management committee (Kane, 2011). The difficulties faced by managers in seeking to engage in environmental sustainability are explained mainly by the degree of complexity of environmental issues, managers' lack of environmental concern, and their tendency to focus on their main tasks (Andersson & Bateman, 2000).

7.1.4   Individual Level

A cursory glance at research on obstacles to the adoption of environmental behaviors shows that most scholars implicitly agree on the fact that individuals tend to formalize their own obstacles, the main roots of which are of an axiological, cognitive, moral, or attitudinal nature.

Gifford (2011) categorized the psychological barriers impacting individual decisions to engage in environmentally responsible behavior, such as limiting greenhouse gas-emitting behavior in the context of climate change. To do so, Gifford proposed a list of 29 psychological barriers grouped into the following seven categories: ideologies (i.e., people are confident that mankind has an appropriate solution for environmental problems); limited cognition (i.e., having a poor understanding of environmental issues); comparisons with others (i.e., individuals are prone to behave like members of their reference group); sunk costs (i.e., it is easier for people to avoid changing their habits and behaviors than to change them); discredence (i.e., those who raise alarm about environmental issues are not trustworthy); perceived risks (i.e., in comparison to maintaining one's standard behaviors, behavioral change is perceived as risky); and limited behaviors (i.e., performing only a few environmentally responsible behaviors with little energy). Based on their literature review on pro-environmental behavior in the private sphere, Steg and Vlek (2009) found that motivation, context and habit are the three main factors that positively influence individual environmental behaviors. Conversely, there is an assumption that apathetic individuals with little concern for environmental matters are likely to express the following traits: low moral concern such that the individual tends to place his or her immediate interests above environmental values; a lack of concern about social approval when not engaging in ecological efforts; failure to search for solutions when appropriate facilities are lacking; and cognitive reasoning, according to which past behaviors tend to explain current behaviors toward the environment (e.g., if my habit is not to recycle, I tend to be consistent, regardless of the situation or circumstances).

These obstacles can be distinguished by considering intrapersonal processes ("between process") and interpersonal processes ("within process"). Cervone (2005) discussed the usefulness of the distinction for research on personality. In line with Cervone, the aim is to determine the extent to which the individual variations apparent within a given group of individuals reflect the mental system of each of its members. By extension, intrapersonal processes account, based on moral, cognitive, and axiological grounds, for the roots or origins of the behavioral dynamics of a given individual relative to a given object. Interpersonal processes imply considering the variables associated with other people with whom that individual regularly interacts. These interactions are assessed in terms of quantity (for example, the amount of contact over the course of a day's work) and quality (for example, the degree to which interactions involve reciprocity). The split between within and between processes seems appropriate for categorizing obstacles to the adoption of pro-environmental behaviors.

7.1.5   Within Process

A lack of knowledge, personal skills, and individual competencies in relation to environmental matters is often viewed as an obstacle (see Chapter 8). However, it is important to distinguish between basic and technical knowledge here. In discussing the implementation of environmental training practices, Milliman and Clair (1996) noted that a lack of basic skills (such as reading and writing) or a poor grasp of simple numerical operations may also create obstacles in cases where individuals struggle to understand the subtleties of a text and the associated nuances. To many people, functional illiteracy may seem to be a marginal explanation or even an exaggerated factor to be treated as an epiphenomenon when the unit of analysis is the workplace. The issue extends to our understanding of the content and meaning of the signs used to guide people in making the right environmental choices. For example, Price and Pitt

(2012) noted that "signs for recycling facilities have an important role but attention to the possible misinterpretation of signs is a factor to consider (p. 624).

7.1.6   Between-Process

Group values that are not strongly adhered to by team members and lack of engagement by others, whether leaders or colleagues, can act as obstacles (Plank, 2011). Other obstacles may involve the nature of the work carried out and lack of feedback about whether or not employees perform their job well (Plank, 2011). A perceived lack of resources devoted to environmental matters may reduce the capacity or tendency of employees to engage in eco-friendly behavior on the job (Tudor, Barr, & Gilg, 2008). Costs related to energy consumption have been found to act as an obstacle since energy appears to be more diffuse in work settings than in domestic settings and may explain why employees fail to engage in eco-friendly behaviors at work by, for example, seeking to reduce energy consumption or increasing paper recycling (Manika, Wells, Gregory-Smith, & Gentry, 2015; Siero, Boon, Kok, & Siero, 1989). Finally, it has recently been found that employees may refrain from behaving in eco-friendly ways when they believe that their employer has not adhered to the terms of the psychological contract (Paillé & Mejia-Morelos, 2014).

From an employee point of view, the list of obstacles is especially long. Classifying obstacles based on the four levels set out above provides a way of rethinking how they exert influence on employees' environmental behaviors. Gaspar, Palma-Oliveira, and Corral-Verdugo (2010) argued that "people can construct their own reality through social and cognitive processes and thus, some aspect of people's environment can work as a behavioral barrier if people perceive that aspect in such a way" (p. 272). Gaspar et al. emphasized the importance of individuals' perception of the characteristics of their immediate environment. These characteristics act as obstacles structured according to their degree of materiality, from the most concrete to the most abstract. The degree of materiality can be based on the different levels described above. The position taken by Gaspar et al. implicitly raises the question of the structure of reality in the mental space of individuals, a question to which the authors provide no real answer.

To better understand how different obstacles exert varying degrees of influence on employees, a conceptual tool is needed to go further in understanding how limitations affect individuals according to circumstances. Here, it is useful to draw on field theory as developed and refined by Lewin between and 1930s and the 1950s. The value of field theory for the study of environmental behaviors has recently been underlined by Tudor and Dutra (2018) and Endrejat and Kauffeld (2018) in research on behavioral change. The Lewinian theoretical framework also provides appropriate conceptual foundations for reconfiguring obstacles in the mental space of individuals.

7.2   AN APPROACH TO ENVIRONMENTAL OBSTACLES USING LEWINIAN FIELD THEORY

7.2.1   *Lewinian Field: Definition and Fundamental Principles*

7.2.1.1   *Defining the Notion of Lewinian Field*

In its initial version, the concept of Lewinian field represents, alongside Group Dynamics, Action Research and the 3-Step model of change, one of the four components of the general framework developed by Lewin for the study of social dynamics as a whole (Burns, 2004). The value of field theory here is that it points to various connections with border theory as developed by Clark (2000). For example, the principles of border impermeability or flexibility represent significant points of convergence between field theory and border theory. However, one significant difference is that, in field theory, borders are viewed as the expression of more or less conscious psychologized representations, whereas in border theory they are perceived by individuals as a reality which, though subjective, alters the objective conditions of their relation to domains.

Lewinian field theory is associated with a unique terminology drawn from the vocabulary of the physical sciences. According to Burns (2004), this largely accounts for the abstruse nature of the developments subtending field theory, which remains the least well understood area of Lewin's work. However, as noted by Burnes and Cooke (2013), the full meaning of the terminology borrowed by Lewin can only be grasped if we remind ourselves that Lewin's aim was to embed psychology in a solid scientific paradigm. The use of ideas and concepts drawn from the physical sciences is not really accompanied by any attempt to adapt them to the field of social science. Indeed, the main deficiency of Lewin's approach is precisely its lack of pedagogy. His determination to reduce concepts to mathematical expressions is often given as a reason for both the luke-warm reception given to this aspect of his work and the relative success of field theory among the community of researchers in psychology (Burnes & Cooke, 2013).

Lewin (1951) defined the concept of field as "the totality of coexisting and interdependent forces" (p. 240). The totality of forces corresponds to interconnected events that determine "behavior b at time t which is a function of situation S at time t" (Lewin, 1943, p. 297). The situation refers to the *Life Space*, encompassing the individual and their psychological environment. The life space corresponds to the totality of forces that can influence a person's behavior at a given time. The totality of forces and characteristics situated outside the life space constitutes the *Physical World*. Here, the notion of "fact" should be understood to mean any type of event (or variable), whether tangible (a concrete object) or intangible (for example, a belief), that may influence an individual's behavior at a given point in time (Hall, Lindzey, & Campbell, 1998). It follows that a behavior may be understood outside the situation (S) and time (T) in which it is exhibited or performed.

7.2.1.2   Time and Space

In a Lewinian field, a behavior is contextualized in both time and space (Lewin, 1943). The spatial and temporal contextualization of behavior implies that, except for observations conducted in a closed system, a given behavior cannot be linked to a past or future behavior. Lastly, Lewin introduced the principle of contemporaneity to specify the role of time in shaping behaviors. Here, a distinction is drawn between the psychological past and the psychological future. Without explicitly saying so, Lewin appears to operate on the basis of a Bergsonian approach to time and its effects on current behavior. From a field theory perspective, behavior can be affected by the subjective dimension of time since personal experiences situated in the past can continue to influence behavior in the present. The future may be associated with the hope that enables an individual to project themselves into the future.

Finally, Lewin contends that present time compresses past and future time. Past and future time are thus inherent elements of an individual's psychological field. Therefore, to understand the motives of present behavior, we need to take into account both past experiences and future expectations. Only the situation changes, not the behavior, implying that the analysis of individual motivations for behavior first requires under-standing the factors underlying the variability of the physical and social environment in which an individual operates. In an extreme case that may be regarded as hypothetical, a situation which remains unchanged provides no basis for influencing behavior. As a significant factor, the action of change must relate to the structure of the psychological field, not to the elements of the individual's mental structure. It is only once the structure of that field is modified that it is possible to put in place the conditions required for a change in behavior.

Based on these various elements, a Lewinian field involves three funda-mental principles. The first is the principle of *proximity/distance*, which explains the degree of influence between two events. Two proximate events are likely to influence each other to a greater extent than two remote events. The second principle is the principle of *firmness/weakness* materialized by the porosity of borders between two events. The third principle is the principle of *fluidity/roughness* whereby the degree of influ-ence of an event (or "force") remote from another depends on the ease with which another event acts or does not act as an intermediary.

7.2.2   The Structure of Obstacles According to the Principles of the Lewinian Field

7.2.2.1   Topology as Metaphor

The spatial representation of facts for understanding a behavior of interest is approached by Lewin in topological terms (Hall et al., 1998). In a Lewinian context, the idea of *topology* should be understood as the way in which the properties of the psychological field are distributed and positioned relative to each other in the form of a psychologized spatial representation.

Figure 7.1 proposes to adopt these general principles. Each poten-tial obstacle to the adoption of an environmental behavior is located and associated with a region of the psychological field. Consistent with the approach adopted in this book, the reference point is the subjective perspective of the individual. Obstacles and their potential influence on the adoption of an environmental behavior are therefore examined from an employee point of view. Obstacles located in the *Within* region are psychologically closer to the individual than those situated in the *Legis-lation* region. Here, location is not to be understood in physical terms but in terms of the capacity to influence. For example, if environmental

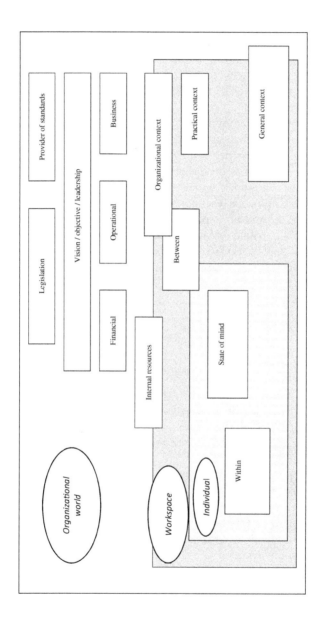

Fig. 7.1   Representation of obstacles based on the model of Lewinian field theory

legislation is not applied by an organization out of choice, it automatically represents a major obstacle with a potentially strong contingent effect on an employee concerned about environmental matters.

In what follows, I propose to maintain this idea. The main aim is to go some way toward providing a coherent explanation of how obstacles hamper employee environmental engagement. Lastly, for reasons largely related to the need to adapt the Lewinian principles to the organizational domain, in Fig. 7.1 I have opted to replace the terms "physical world," "living space," "personality," and "facts" with the following terms: "organizational level," "work environment," "individual," and "obstacles." Based on one of the structuring characteristics of a Lewinian field, through interlocking, individuals are embedded in their work space, which is itself embedded in the organizational level. The individual, work, environmental, and organizational levels are separated by boundaries of varying permeability. Depending on their degree of permeability, boundaries cause obstacles to play a greater or lesser role in shaping environmental behaviors.

7.2.2.2 Weak and Strong Situations

I also contend that the permeability of boundaries depends to a great extent on circumstances and situations. In the Lewinian approach to fields, the situation is a central characteristic. My contention is that boundaries operate as obstacles that generate constraints or barriers that prevent employees from performing pro-environmental behaviors. In addition, boundaries are either material or immaterial and are perceived as being more or less permeable (see Chapter 6).

Mischel (1977) speculated that "situations" may be weak or strong depending on the degree of goal clarity, (un)shared objectives, and the presence or lack of relevant skills and habits to perform the behavior of interest. The distinction between strong and weak situations may be helpful in shaping the discussion of how boundaries operate as obstacles. Strong situations "lead everyone to construe the particular events the same way, induce uniform expectancies regarding the most appropriate response pattern, provide adequate incentives for the performance of that response pattern and require skills that everyone has to the same extent" (p. 347). By contrast, weak situations "do not generate uniform expectancies concerning desired behavior, do not offer sufficient incentives for its performance, or fail to provide the learning conditions required for successful genesis of behavior" (p. 276). The implication is that a strong situation arises when organizational members have the same pattern of reasoning, share the same objectives and values, and hold the adequate skills at their own level to achieve these shared objectives.

- A strong situation concerns members who share the same view of ecology. In this case, ecology is a familiar issue for all members. The notion implies two individuals with a significant interest in, or concern for, environmental matters, but also two individuals with a limited interest in such matters. In both cases, the common denominator is convergence of opinion. Another implication is that a discrepancy regarding these previous characteristics may give rise to a weak situation that can have a detrimental effect on individual behaviors.
- A weak situation concerns all cases involving a divergence of opinion or a gap in skills, competencies or know-how. In this case, ecological matters are not a familiar topic for at least one of the two parties involved.

Weak and strong situations provide a useful and relevant basis for illustrating how and why obstacles play a critical role in shaping the relationship between familiar partners (e.g., an immediate supervisor and their subordinates, coworkers in a team, colleagues working in different services, departments or divisions, and so on) in a context where an (un)familiar issue occurs, such as corporate greening.

7.2.3   Some Evidence from the Environmental Literature

The principles of proximity/distance, fluidity/roughness and firmness/weakness are important characteristics of a Lewinian field. In what follows, I propose to illustrate the action of these three principles on employees by drawing on a range of evidence.

7.2.3.1   Proximity/Distance

In a Lewinian field, regions are interconnected, meaning that the sources of obstacles are interconnected from a topological point of view in the individual's mental space. This has a significant impact on the capacity of an individual to act pro-environmentally simply because the mutual influence of sources is not necessarily linked to their degree of proximity. The proximity/distance principle enables an individual to locate the relative position of each obstacle by taking into account both their source and their degree of influence. Obstacles at the institutional and organizational levels are distant, whereas obstacles at the managerial and individual levels are close. From an employee perspective, proximate sources of obstacles in the mental space of an individual may not mutually influence each other. On the other hand, remote sources of obstacles may be interconnected and exert influence on environmental behavior. The key factor is the degree of firmness/weakness of the boundary separating different sources of obstacles. Here, the role performed by border crossers is critical (for a reminder, see Chapter 6).

This means, for example, that a lack of environmental vision at the organizational level or a lack of environmental leadership at a managerial level can impact the individual as an obstacle creating a barrier or a constraint. Research in this area has emphasized the role of leadership in predicting workplace pro-environmental behaviors. A number of different leadership styles have been examined in the recent environmental literature. For example, Graves, Sarkis, and Zhu (2013) investigated the role of environmental transformational leadership on employees' motivation to engage in pro-environmental behaviors. They suggested that when supervisors base their leadership on "a clear and coherent environmental vision for the area of responsibility" (p. 82), the latter may be perceived by their subordinates as an inspiring model by giving them the necessary motivation to make efforts beyond their job duties that contribute to environmental sustainability. The main findings of the study by Graves, Sarkis, and Zhu were that while environmental transformational leadership positively influences PEBs through autonomous motivation, it also moderates the effect of external motivation on PEBs such that under low environmental leadership external motivation tends to decrease PEBs and increase PEBs under high environmental leadership.

In a given sector of activity, the environmental vision of an organization informs rival organizations of its environmental leadership. For example, an organization with strong environmental leadership can inspire competitors in the sector to adopt, through a process of imitation, a similar strategic approach in order to achieve a competitive advantage over rivals in the sector. This principle is known as the mimetic effect, which refers "to the tendency of individuals […] inclined to imitate the successful practices of others around them" (Zhang, Wang, Yin, & Su, 2012). The mimetic effect can act as a driver demonstrating an interest in environmental matters on the part of the senior management of an organization which may face internal obstacles at the point of implementation. Zhu and Geng (2013) studied a sample of manufacturers to determine the extent to which external drivers (e.g., environmental regulations, the environmental preferences of customers or consumers, and the mimetic environmental practices of successful competitors in the sector) and internal obstacles (e.g., excessively high costs, such as eco-design costs, lack of commitment from senior managers, low energy-saving awareness among workers, no clear statement of responsibilities across different departments, lack of collection and analysis of material/energy flow data) determine the introduction of a saving and emission reduction (ESER) program encouraged at the institutional level by the local authorities.

Their results indicate, on the one hand, that imitation is the most important factor driving the decision to establish an energy consumption reduction program and, on the other, that internal obstacles impede sustainable purchasing but not sustainable customer cooperation in achieving energy saving and emission reduction targets. Unfortunately, internal obstacles were envisaged as a whole, and no details are provided about the actual role of the most influential obstacles when considered in isolation. However, the loadings reported by Zhu and Geng (2013) give a rough idea of the internal obstacles identified by the respondents by ranking them from the most influential to the least influential (see Table 3 in the study of Zhu and Geng). In descending order, we have:

- lack of internal expertise on environmental issues;
- lack of internal technological resources;
- low ESER awareness among workers;
- lack of R&D capability on ESER;
- no clear statement for responsibilities among different departments;
- lack of capabilities to solve internal ESER issues;
- high cost of using environmental packaging;
- high cost of producing ESER products;
- excessive costs (eco-design, etc.);
- lack of collection and analysis of material/energy flow data;
- no commitment from senior managers;
- no significant benefit (esp. short-term benefit);
- excessively high disposable cost for hazardous wastes.

In summary, the study by Zhu and Geng (2013) showed that the environmental vision can encounter a whole range of obstacles operating at different levels within an organization and that, ultimately, an employee motivated by environmental concerns may personally be confronted with obstacles that operate, depending on the circumstances, as barriers if their work premises are not adapted to protecting the environment or as constraints if, at their own personal level, the leeway needed to perform simple actions exists but is constrained by a limited capacity to act in environmentally friendly ways.

7.2.3.2   Fluidity/Roughness

This principle involves an intermediate region that acts as a connector between two regions. The connection between two remote regions is ensured or affected according to the capacity of the intermediate region to interfere. The application of this principle to the question of internal obstacles suggests, for example, that notwithstanding the absence of obstacles at the institutional level, employees may be hindered by the emergence of new obstacles at other levels. Put differently, the introduction of the conditions required for greening at a global level is no guarantee that employees will adopt ecologically responsible behaviors at their own level. A good example of this is the study by Zhu and Geng (2013), the results of which (discussed above) provide evidence for the role of internal obstacles at different organizational levels. Tudor et al. (2008) examined the individual motivations underlying waste management in a health organization. Their study found that despite the existence of environmental management practices, the level of employee engagement in medical waste recycling practices can be explained by a lack of resources and, more specifically, by a shortage of staff dedicated to the implementation of environmental practices.

The principle of roughness/fluidity also suggests that the existence of obstacles at the institutional level may not necessarily have an impact on the ability of employees to adopt pro-environmental behaviors. This can be attributed to the role of immediate supervisor support. Indeed, environmental studies have repeatedly demonstrated the influence of immediate supervisor support on environmental behaviors—not least because, through such support, the immediate supervisor signals their approval of their subordinates' environmental actions. Approval can take many forms, including emotional support (sympathy, listening and caring), instrumental support (material or concrete assistance), informational support (knowledge and advice), and appraisal (giving appropriate feedback) (Rostila, 2011). Immediate supervisors may be impeded in their commitment to support their subordinates in acting responsibly toward the environment. A supervisor who is not supported by their line managers on environmental matters will be faced with a direct obstacle, the effects of which will impact their subordinates. The contexts of strong and weak situations play an important role in this regard.

In the case of a strong situation (mutual understanding and sharing of environmental concerns), subordinates will be faced with a barrier if their actions require their immediate supervisor to be able to provide the resources they need to be environmentally engaged. An immediate supervisor with no real power to protect the environment will have limited room for maneuver, thereby affecting their ability to support subordinates keen to promote greening in their workplace, even if the latter feel that their own supervisor is supported by their organization (Paillé, Amara, & Halilem, 2013). However, if support for actions does not require any specific material resources, simple support practices in the form of encouragement can enable subordinates to overcome day-to-day obstacles (Humphrey, Bord, Hammond, & Mann, 1977).

In the case of a weak situation, the gap between the pro-environmental values held by the immediate supervisor and their subordinate operates as a barrier to action if no material support is provided, such as a lack of appropriate recipients or containers for recycling. Environmental studies conducted in work settings have reported that difficulties in accessing appropriate facilities tend to be experienced by employees as an obstacle (Price & Pitt, 2012). A lack of environmental support will act as a constraint in cases where the immediate manager does not take into account environmental concerns in managing their subordinates' work. Lamm, Tosti-Kharas, and King (2015) argued that "if employees fear looking like they are wasting company time, a good performance evaluation may trump environmental values" (p. 210). Lack of time is often put forward by employees as an obstacle to environmental engagement (Yuriev, Boiral, Francoeur, & Paillé, 2018).

In another study (Jabbour et al., 2016) conducted in the Brazilian manufacturing sector, the authors found that obstacles at the institutional level (i.e., lack of flexibility in compliance with legal deadlines, difficulties associated with the environmental legislation application and monitoring process, and lack of flexibility in compliance with legal demands) have no influence on the introduction of production practices that respect environmental constraints, while obstacles at the organizational and managerial levels (senior managers' limited environmental awareness, resistance by senior managers to changes in work habits) and at the individual level (limited environmental awareness at the employee level) tend to significantly affect their implementation. Therefore, the introduction of environmentally respectful production practices was found to have a significantly greater effect on environmental performance than on operational performance. In Jabbour et al. (2016), it is interesting to note that the obstacles that were psychologically closest to employees appeared to replace psychologically remote institutional obstacles. Though it is difficult to draw any conclusions, and while they provide no direct evidence, these findings appear to be an indicator of how the principle of roughness/fluidity operates in practice.

7.2.3.3   Firmness/Weakness
In a Lewinian field, the firmness/weakness principle determines the role of boundaries between two regions. Here, the implication is that the degree of influence of obstacles depends on the porosity of borders. In this case too, the immediate manager performs an important role, not least because he or she acts as a border crosser. In discussing the work of Clark in Chapter 6, I noted that boundaries are either symbolic or physical. For example, leading is a way of helping subordinates to cross a symbolic boundary. Robertson and Barling (2013) showed that subordinates are more prone to engage in PEBs when their managers communicate their passion for the environment and behave in environmentally friendly ways. More recently, Afsar, Badir, and Kiani (2016) examined spiritual leadership in the context of environmental sustainability by arguing that this style "is one of the most effective approaches when it comes to influence [sic] the employees to display pro-environmental behavior" (p. 80). The basis for their contention is that the supervisor, through his or her spirituality, helps subordinates to develop their environmental awareness not only for the sake of ensuring a sustainable workplace but also for protecting the environment for future generations. The authors found that spiritual leadership has a positive indirect effect on employee pro-environmental behaviors through workplace spirituality, environmental passion, and intrinsic motivation for those employees who are high both in perceived organizational support and in environmental awareness.

The principle of firmness/weakness can also be expressed among peers. In a study focusing on the role of intervention practices aimed at improving paper recycling practices, Brothers, Krantz, and McClannahan (1994) reported a substantial improvement (from 85 to 94%) in the total amount of recyclable paper being recycled. While recognizing the importance of appropriate facilities and measures, the authors argued that "[t]he addition of these employees increases the significance of the maintenance data, especially because these participants were not present when memos were distributed. Although it is possible that senior colleagues communicated the definition of recyclable paper to these new employees (i.e., in the same way that one might expect them to communicate other policies and procedures), it seems quite likely that local containers were relevant discriminative stimuli for recycling" (p. 157). More recently, Paillé, Amara, and Halilem (2018) showed that mutual support among colleagues determines the conditions under which environmentally friendly behavioral attitudes are disseminated in workplace settings. These studies indicate that the quality of relationships between colleagues tends to act as a catalyst of support and encouragement. Yet, paradoxically, peer encouragement can also generate obstacles. Chen, Chen, Huang, Long, and Li (2017) inferred from their results that individuals who are relatively close in the professional sphere can nonetheless experience verbal prompts and encouragements by their peers to act in environmentally friendly ways as a form of interference resulting in the opposite effect of that intended—i.e., environmental disengagement.

Some concluding remarks

Having an individual belief about the need to care for the environment does not appear to be a sufficient guarantee that people will transfer their goodwill from the private domain to the work domain. Research conducted in organizational settings has also shown that internal obstacles may impede employees' willingness to behave in environmentally friendly ways. In this chapter, the matter was approached from an employee perspective to explain two key ideas. On the one hand, obstacles can be ordered or structured according to different levels: the institutional, organizational, managerial, and individual levels. On the other hand, obstacles are psychologically distributed in the mental space of an employee according to a topological logic characteristic of a Lewinian field. In taking this approach, this chapter provided an original interpretation of the inhibiting effects that constrain the environmental engagement of employees.

REFERENCES

Afsar, B., Badir, Y., & Kiani, U. S. (2016). Linking spiritual leadership and employee pro-environmental behavior: The influence of workplace spirituality, intrinsic motivation, and environmental passion. *Journal of Environmental Psychology, 45*, 79–88.

Anderson, L. M., & Bateman, T. S. (2000). Individual environmental initiative: Championing natural environmental issues in US business organizations. *Academy of Management Journal, 43*(4), 548–570.

Brothers, K. J., Krantz, P. J., & McClannahan, L. E. (1994). Office paper recycling: A function of container proximity. *Journal of Applied Behavior Analysis, 27*(1), 153–160.

Burnes, B., & Cooke, B. (2013). Kurt Lewin's field theory: A review and re-evaluation. *International Journal of Management Reviews, 15*(4), 408–425.

Burns, B. (2004). Kurt Lewin and the planned approach to change: A re-appraisal. *Journal of Management Studies, 41*(6), 977–1002.

Cervone, D. (2005). Personality architecture: Within-person structures and processes. *Annual Review of Psychology, 56*, 423–452.

Chen, H., Chen, F., Huang, X., Long, R., & Li, W. (2017). Are individuals' environmental behavior always consistent?—An analysis based on spatial difference. *Resources, Conservation and Recycling, 125*, 25–36.

Clark, S. C. (2000). Work/family border theory: A new theory of work/family balance. *Human Relations, 53*(6), 747–770.

Cordano, M., & Frieze, I. H. (2000). Pollution reduction preferences of US environmental managers: Applying Ajzen's theory of planned behavior. *Academy of Management Journal, 43*(4), 627–641.

Egri, C. P., & Herman, S. (2000). Leadership in the North American environmental sector: Values, leadership styles, and contexts of environmental leaders and their organizations. *Academy of Management Journal, 43*(4), 571–604.

Endrejat, P. C., & Kauffeld, S. (2018). Motivation towards "green" behaviour at the workplace: Facilitating employee pro-environmental behaviour through participatory interventions. In *Research handbook on employee pro-environmental behaviour*. Cheltenham: Edward Elgar Publishing.

Gaspar, R., Palma-Oliveira, J. M., & Corral-Verdugo, V. (2010). Why do people fail to act? Situational barriers and constraints on ecological behavior. In *Psychological approaches to sustainability: Current trends in research, theory and practice* (pp. 269–294). New York: Nova Science Publishers.

Gifford, R. (2011). The dragons of inaction: Psychological barriers that limit climate change mitigation and adaptation. *American Psychologist, 66*(4), 290–302.

Graves, L. M., Sarkis, J., & Zhu, Q. (2013). How transformational leadership and employee motivation combine to predict employee proenvironmental behaviors in China. *Journal of Environmental Psychology, 35,* 81–91.

Hall, C. S., Lindzey, G., & Campbell, J. B. (1998). *Theories of personality.* New York: Wiley.

Humphrey, C. R., Bord, R. J., Hammond, M. M., & Mann, S. H. (1977). Attitudes and conditions for cooperation in a paper recycling program. *Environment and Behavior, 9*(1), 107–124.

Jabbour, C. J. C., de Sousa Jabbour, A. B. L., Govindan, K., De Freitas, T. P., Soubihia, D. F., Kannan, D., & Latan, H. (2016). Barriers to the adoption of green operational practices at Brazilian companies: Effects on green and operational performance. *International Journal of Production Research, 54*(10), 3042–3058.

Kane, A. (2011). Green recruitment, development and engagement. In *Going green: The psychology of sustainability in the workplace.* Leicester: The British Psychological Society.

Kollmuss, A., & Agyeman, J. (2002). Mind the gap: Why do people act environmentally and what are the barriers to pro-environmental behavior? *Environmental Education Research, 8*(3), 239–260.

Lamm, E., Tosti-Kharas, J., & King, C. E. (2015). Empowering employee sustainability: Perceived organizational support toward the environment. *Journal of Business Ethics, 128*(1), 207–220.

Lewin, K. (1943). Defining the 'field at a given time'. *Psychological Review, 50*(3), 292.

Lewin, K. (1951). *Field theory in social science: Selected theoretical papers* (D. Cartwright, Ed.). New York: Harper & Brothers.

Lorenzoni, I., Nicholson-Cole, S., & Whitmarsh, L. (2007). Barriers perceived to engaging with climate change among the UK public and their policy implications. *Global Environmental Change, 17*(3–4), 445–459.

Manika, D., Wells, V. K., Gregory-Smith, D., & Gentry, M. (2015). The impact of individual attitudinal and organisational variables on workplace environmentally friendly behaviours. *Journal of Business Ethics, 126*(4), 663–684.

Milliman, J., & Clair, J. (1996). Best environmental HRM practices in the U.S. In W. Wehrmeyer (Ed.), *Greening people: Human resources and environmental management* (pp. 49–73). Sheffield: Greenleaf Publishing.

Mischel, W. (1977). The interaction of person and situation. In *Personality at the crossroads: Current issues in interactional psychology* (pp. 333–352). Hillsdale, NJ: Lawrence Erlbaum Associates.

Paillé, P., Amara, N., & Halilem, N. (2018). Greening the workplace through social sustainability among co-workers. *Journal of Business Research, 89,* 305–312.

Paillé, P., Boiral, O., & Chen, Y. (2013). Linking environmental management practices and organizational citizenship behaviour for the environment: A social exchange perspective. *The International Journal of Human Resource Management, 24*(18), 3552–3575.

Paillé, P., & Mejía-Morelos, J. H. (2014). Antecedents of pro-environmental behaviours at work: The moderating influence of psychological contract breach. *Journal of Environmental Psychology, 38,* 124–131.

Plank, R. (2011). Green behaviour: Barriers, facilitators and the role of attributions. In *Going green: The psychology of sustainability in the workplace* (pp. 47–58). Leicester: British Psychological Society.

Price, S., & Pitt, M. (2012). The influence of facilities and environmental values on recycling in an office environment. *Indoor and Built Environment, 21*(5), 622–632.

Robertson, J. L., & Barling, J. (2013). Greening organizations through leaders' influence on employees' pro-environmental behaviors. *Journal of Organizational Behavior, 34*(2), 176–194.

Robertson, J. L., & Barling, J. (Eds.). (2015). *The psychology of green organizations.* New York, NY: Oxford University Press.

Rostila, M. (2011). The facets of social capital. *Journal for the Theory of Social Behaviour, 41*(3), 308–326.

Schmit, M. J., Fegley, S., Esen, E., Schramm, J., & Tomassetti, A. (2012). Human resource management efforts for environmental sustainability. In S. E. Jackson, D. S. Ones, & S. Dilchert (Eds.), *Managing human resource for environmental sustainability.* San Francisco, CA: Jossey-Bass.

Siero, S., Boon, M., Kok, G., & Siero, F. (1989). Modification of driving behavior in a large transport organization: A field experiment. *Journal of Applied Psychology, 74*(3), 417.

Steg, L., & Vlek, C. (2009). Encouraging pro-environmental behaviour: An integrative review and research agenda. *Journal of Environmental Psychology, 29*(3), 309–317.

Tudor, T. L., Barr, S. W., & Gilg, A. W. (2008). A novel conceptual framework for examining environmental behavior in large organizations: A case study of the Cornwall National Health Service (NHS) in the United Kingdom. *Environment and Behavior, 40*(3), 426–450.

Tudor, T., & Dutra, C. (2018). Embedding pro-environmental behaviour change in large organisations: Perspectives on the complexity of the challenge. In *Research handbook on employee pro-environmental behaviour.* Cheltenham: Edward Elgar Publishing.

Yuriev, A., Boiral, O., Francoeur, V., & Paillé, P. (2018). Overcoming the barriers to pro-environmental behaviors in the workplace: A systematic review. *Journal of Cleaner Production, 182,* 379–394.

Zhang, B., Wang, Z., Yin, J., & Su, L. (2012). CO2 emission reduction within Chinese iron & steel industry: Practices, determinants and performance. *Journal of Cleaner Production, 33,* 167–178.

Zhu, Q., & Geng, Y. (2013). Drivers and barriers of extended supply chain practices for energy saving and emission reduction among Chinese manufacturers. *Journal of Cleaner Production, 40,* 6–12.

Zibarras, L., & Ballinger, C. (2011). Promoting environmental behaviour in the workplace: A survey of UK organisations. In *Going green: The psychology of sustainability in the workplace* (pp. 84–90). Leicester: The British Psychological Society.

CHAPTER 8

Greening the Workplace Through Employees: An Integrative Model

Abstract This chapter continues the discussion begun in previous chapters. The existing literature focuses mainly on the individual, managerial, and organizational conditions governing the adoption of pro-environmental behaviors in the workplace. Alongside this, albeit to a lesser extent, part of the literature has also acknowledged the existence of non-environmental behaviors by seeking to describe their causes. This chapter presents a new integrative model designed to bring together pro-environmental and non-environmental behaviors, pressures, constraints, and incentives to workplace greening.

Keywords Integrative model · Environmental inaction · In(appropriate) action · Decision-making pathways

8.1 Development of the Model: Theoretical Foundations

8.1.1 Structuring Elements

Very few models have sought to describe the cognitive and attitudinal factors of inertia and inaction alongside (in)appropriate environmental behaviors in workplace settings. Figure 8.1 offers a visual representation of the proposed integrative model incorporating all three elements.

© The Author(s) 2020
P. Paillé, *Greening the Workplace*,
https://doi.org/10.1007/978-3-030-58388-0_8

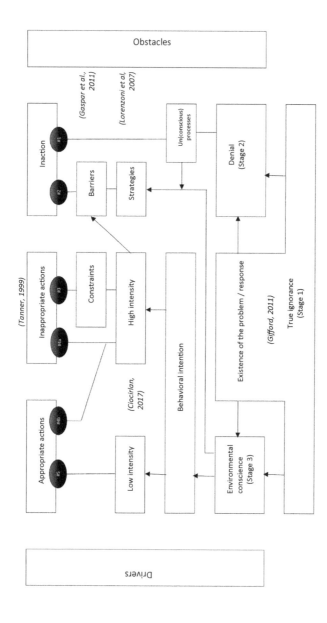

Fig. 8.1 The integrative model

The model essentially involves using and integrating a range of structuring elements drawn from a series of studies published over the course of the last twenty years (Ciocirlan, 2017; Gaspar, 2013; Gifford, 2011; Lorenzoni, Nicholson-Cole, & Whitmarsh, 2007; Tanner, 1999). In what follows, I will be providing a brief description of these structuring elements. Each study proposes more substantial developments that will be introduced and used at a later stage when a range of alternatives leading employees to adopt (or not adopt) pro-environmental behaviors in the workplace will be considered and described.

8.1.1.1   *Ignorance, Denial, and Awareness*

The first structuring element of the model is provided by Gifford (2011). In the opening lines of his paper, Gifford strongly suggests that genuine ignorance of the causes and consequences of climate change is a powerful factor of inertia that serves to limit any type of action likely to result in a positive contribution to the environment at an individual level. Gifford indicates that while ignorance tends to confirm and maintain an individual in an attitude of denial toward environmental matters, ignorance does not definitively confine the individual to inaction and inertia. Indeed, in some circumstances, ignorance can give way to environmental awareness, leading individuals to take action in order to limit environmentally harmful behaviors.

8.1.1.2   *Individual Denial Strategies*

The second structuring element is provided in a paper by Lorenzoni et al. (2007) in which the authors list a range of factors that inhibit the action of individuals despite their desire to act in environmentally friendly ways. These inhibitors are categorized according to whether their origin is linked to a perceived individual inability or to perceived social and institutional obstacles or impediments. In their study, some factors of inhibition at the individual level are seen as individual strategies whereby individuals are able to justify the reasons for their environmental inaction. From this point of view, individual strategies offer a means of understanding the consequences of the process of denial.

8.1.1.3   *Obstacles, Constraints, and Barriers*

The third structuring element is drawn from a conceptual study by Gaspar (2013) in which obstacles to the adoption of pro-environmental behaviors are examined with the aim of going beyond merely descriptive explanations in favor of a model of reasoning that focuses on the processes by which an individual comes to behave in an environmentally friendly (or unfriendly) way. Gaspar makes a distinction between the notions of obstacle, barrier and constraint, the three terms generally used to describe the factors that hamper or affect the ability or willingness of individuals to adopt pro-environmental behaviors. He proposes to define an obstacle according to whether it constitutes a barrier or a constraint. The difference between the two terms revolves around the scale or magnitude of individual responses. A barrier inhibits action while a constraint interferes in individual decisions. The term "obstacle" is used as an umbrella term to denote the general idea of a hindrance or impediment to individual action. Far from being a mere semantic trick, Gaspar's proposal provides a way of better understanding the reasons why individuals force themselves to act in environmentally friendly ways.

8.1.1.4   Required Intensity
The fourth structuring element is provided in a study by Ciocirlan (2017). The aim of the paper is to refine the definition of pro-environmental behaviors by introducing a set of characteristics so far neglected in the reference literature. Among these characteristics, Ciocirlan introduces the idea of the level of intensity as an indicator for assessing the degree of risk when individuals engage in environmental behaviors. Individual risk is a function of the following three characteristics: (1) the degree of uncertainty associated with achieving results, (2) the resulting individual costs, and (3) the individual consequences borne by the individual promoting these behaviors.

8.1.1.5   (In)appropriate Nature of Individual Actions
The final structuring element is provided by Tanner (1999). Tanner's paper applies the premises of ipsative theory to driving habits. The theory posits that while individuals may have a generally positive attitude toward a singular behavior, they may be led to make choices which, in some cases, do not altogether reflect their initial intention because of a perceived lack of relevant alternatives. Depending on the combination of these various factors, individuals will tend toward inaction or engage in appropriate or inappropriate behavior.

8.1.2   Prelude to Individual Decision-Making Pathways

The integrative model proposes to explain employee willingness to engage in (in)appropriate actions and their propensity toward inaction. The various structuring elements described above underpin six individual decision-ambling pathways. Each of these pathways proposes to explain how individuals behave from an environmental point of view in workplace settings depending on how they perceive, decode and interpret the characteristics of their organizational context.

Two studies will be used to develop the foundations upon which I propose to formalize decision-making pathways in an environmental context. Ohtomo and Hirose (2007) sought to explain decision-making as a response to a social context, while Amel, Manning, and Scott (2009) set out to provide an account of decision-making in terms of cognitive processes.

8.1.2.1   The Individual Significance of Contextual Constraints

Ohtomo and Hirose (2007) posited that a pro-environmental behavior is theoretically influenced by two distinct decisional processes. The first process is attitudinal intention, which combines the idea of personal environmental concern and normative injunction, i.e., the perceived judgment of members of the relevant social group in the event of inaction. The second process is perceptual and involves a combination of the prototypical image, i.e. the mental representation of a person who adopts a socially undesirable behavior (in the case of the study, a person who does not recycle), and the descriptive norm, i.e., the alignment of the individual with the dominant behaviors of the reference group (friends, colleagues, etc.). Based on an examination of the individual motivation to recycle, the main finding of Ohtomo and Hirose (2007) was that "prosocial motivations to perform eco-friendly behavior are at odds with pro-self motivations to accept eco-unfriendly behavior" (p. 123). One of the implications of their study is that a socially (un)desirable behavior may be (non)intentional and be explained by the social characteristics of the context. Put differently, the context prevails over action. For example, the results of a study by Ohtomo and Hirose (2007) suggest that in a context in which recycling is neither valued nor encouraged, the intention to recycle may not trigger recycling behavior. By contrast, in a context in which recycling is valued and encouraged, an individual may adopt recycling behaviors in spite of their intention not to recycle (this situation also raises the problem of the persistence of behaviors over time). By extension, what this implies is that, in a given situation, an individual may (or may not) adopt a pro-environmental behavior that is inconsistent with their actual intention by accepting a choice that does not reflect their actual decision-making.

8.1.2.2   The Power of Individual Routines

Focusing on decision-making routines, Amel et al. (2009) explained why, against a backdrop of information overload that provides numerous opportunities for refining one's knowledge and improving one's skills and know-how, there is much evidence of ecological behaviors that are not consistent with the degree of environmental awareness reported by individuals. According to Amel et al., in a given situation and faced with a range of possible choices, an individual will tend to choose the least constraining option. The implication is that an individual will tend to prefer the choice that impacts their comfort the least. The routinization of decisions will tend to favor one behavioral action more than others, however difficult it may be to justify it to oneself and others. Finally, Amel et al. (2009) suggested that the routinization of our daily actions prevails over the sense of responsibility toward the environment.

Based on the two studies discussed above, in a context of environmentally responsible behavior, the evidence suggests that individuals are required to navigate between behavioral inertia and contextual pressures.

8.2   Development of the Model: Integration

8.2.1   Stage 1. Ignorance: Its Reasons and Effects

Gifford (2011) argued that ignorance strongly determines an individual's ability to make efforts to minimize their carbon footprint in their day-to-day life. Van de Poel (2011) proposed to define ignorance as a "situation in which we do not even know what could go wrong, resulting in unknown hazards" (p. 285). Ignorance may stem from a lack of objective knowledge about a particular fact or phenomenon but may also be explained by deliberate short-sightedness designed to conceal a reality which, though possible, is difficult to conceptualize. The key role of individual knowledge is a recurring theme in the environmental literature. The level of knowledge can help or hamper individuals in making the link between their understanding of the issues associated with environmental matters and their efforts to minimize their impact on the environment. Whether total or partial, ignorance has many explanations. In any event, it cannot be solely attributed to an individual's level of education, nor is it correlated to the level of available information.

In a study focusing on the reasons why individuals limit their efforts to combat climate change in everyday life, Lorenzoni et al. (2007) showed that inertia stems from a blindness justified by the difficulty faced by respondents in materializing the harmful consequences of climate change, a process seen as occurring over the long term. Official government and international bodies publish reports that often include forecasts and projections over long periods. For example, the report of the 48th session of the Intergovernmental Panel on Climate Change held on October 6, 2018 in Incheon (Republic of Korea) includes the following sentence: "Global warming is likely to reach 1.5°C between 2030 and 2052 if it continues to increase at the current rate" (p. 4). This excerpt contains two key items of information that perfectly illustrate the reasons why it can be difficult for some individuals to grasp the scale of the effects associated with climate change.

- The first relates to the average increase in global temperatures on Earth. A piece of information such as this may lead to an erroneous understanding based on a perception that short-term variations in a given location are greater than the average increase expected over the long term. The principle of the "local effect" (Li, Johnson, & Zaval, 2011) may, in this case, contribute to difficulties in understanding. Studies suggest that the immediate experience of perceived temperature variability is a more significant factor in shaping individual perceptions of the reality of climate change (Zaval, Keenan, Johnson, & Weber, 2014). What this suggests is that, for individuals, the informational content of this type of information is particularly weak.

- The second item of information offers scenarios by providing indications about temporary occurrence. At the time of publication of the report, the lower bound was set at 12 years, while the upper bound was set at around 25 years. This corroborates one of the observations of Lorenzoni et al. (2007), according to which, at the individual level, climate change poses threats which, for many people, remain difficult to conceptualize or substantiate because they are perceived as being remote in time.

Lorenzoni et al. (2007) also showed that a lack of knowledge is sometimes explained by how difficult it can be to find relevant information (Lack of knowledge about where to find information). Knowledge presupposes having access to knowledge media. Information and knowledge can be accessed by many means:

- Academic journals, popular books, and public lectures can be used by anyone to access the very latest knowledge.
- Major international agencies and NGOs usually provide access to reports and summary notes, which anyone can download for free.
- The written press, television, radio and, more recently, tablets and smartphones also play an important role. In this respect, it is interesting to note that the ownership rate globally has been constantly increasing in recent years. According to the Statistica website, in 2020 nearly 2.9 billion people throughout the world used a smartphone.
- An increasing number of celebrities from the worlds of politics and entertainment are becoming involved in the cause of climate change, acting as opinion leaders. Documentaries such as those produced by Leonardo DiCaprio (*Before the Flood*, 2016) and directed by Al Gore (*An Inconvenient Truth*, 2005; *An Inconvenient Sequel*, 2017) are aired on TV and are sometimes available online.

In other words, there is a huge amount of widely available information about climate issues. The forms and media used allow for an ever-wider audience to be reached. Therefore, on the face of it, it seems difficult to argue that ignorance can be explained by a lack of available information. However, there is also a cognitive cost associated with access reflected, paradoxically, by an overabundance of information, further complicating the process of forming a clear opinion about a subject as complex as climate change insofar as the matter involves numerous interpretive frameworks.

The sources of ignorance are also sometimes to be found in the production of academic knowledge and its dissemination among a specific audience or public. Research produces knowledge that requires specific processing operations before being disseminated among the reference community. When knowledge leaves the strictly academic domain to reach out to the general public, a process of popularization is needed to make research findings intelligible. The challenge is to pare academic communication down to its simplest form without thereby reducing its informative quality. The acquisition of knowledge can be disrupted by another key factor. The same object of study is sometimes examined by researchers operating in different disciplines. A good example is the question of sustainable development, an umbrella term covering three main fields (the environmental, social, and economic fields) of interest to researchers working in a wide range of disciplines and exploring an almost infinite number of issues. These fields are often compartmentalized, with little overlap between them. For example, business research in the environmental field concerns management, accounting, marketing, supply chain management, strategy, and many other areas. In addition, each of these fields is structured around specialized academic events (workshops, conferences, etc.). Finally, methods of inquiry, concepts, and approaches also differ profoundly between disciplines. These divergences add an additional layer of cacophony, causing the messages that academics wish to convey to become inaudible.

The structure and organization of research can sometimes create its own obstacles despite the fact that it should, as noted above, facilitate understanding of complex phenomena and thereby contribute directly to raising environmental awareness among the greatest possible number. Research is, by necessity, a slow process that is not simply temporal but also requires a consensus to emerge among the reference community before a phenomenon is considered to be an established fact in accordance with the structuring elements of a paradigm at a given time. By their very nature, research activities generate results that crystallize discussions around specific points which, though important to researchers (and rightly so), can seem futile to the general public.

Academic research activities generate knowledge that forms part of a more or less long-lasting paradigm. Existing paradigms are designed to be challenged by the emergence of new paradigms that provide more refined solutions to the issues under study. The history of science provides much evidence of this process. For example, it would be difficult for a contemporary physicist to offer an explanation of the universe based on Aristotle's geocentric model. Knowledge develops and evolves as new theoretical approaches emerge, analytical methods are improved, and new data are collected. Direct observations reported by researchers can sometimes prove to be contradictory. The retreat of glaciers is an interesting example in this regard. Before-and-after photo montages provide a visual insight into the effects of climate change (this example is drawn from the November 26, 2019 issue of the French regional daily newspaper *Ouest-France*). While overall the process of glacier terminus retreat is taking place at a constant rate, some observations suggest that the size of some glacier snouts in Greenland is tending to decrease at a slower rate (source: D. Altendorf, Sciencepost.fr of 7 April 2019). Although this apparent improvement is presented as temporary, a finding such as this can contribute to feeding doubts about scientific data and information, despite the fact that, in this case, the matter at hand is a local phenomenon that does nothing to undermine the reality of the phenomenon more generally.

In summary, ignorance about environmental matters can be attributed to many factors. Gifford (2011) argued that while environmental igno-rance is one of the main impediments to environmental action combined with, moreover, a strong propensity to favor inaction, it also provides a degree of comfort that enables individuals to overlook any data or infor-mation that may be perceived as disruptive. Amel et al. (2009) contended that encountering an unmanageable volume of information can cause individuals to opt for routine decision-making as a coping mechanism. If we agree with the idea, the implication is that ignorance should be seen not only as a gap in knowledge or knowledge that is difficult to access, but also as something reflective of knowledge that is not mobilized on account of the activation of the decision-making pathways typically mobi-lized to respond to a given situation. In what follows, I propose to explore the effects of this process in the context of environmental inaction.

8.2.2   Stage 2. Beyond Ignorance: Denial and Environmental Inaction

8.2.2.1   The Causes of Inaction

The integrative model posits that what lies at the root of inaction is a personal denial of the issues surrounding environmental questions. Vitousek, Daly, and Heiser (1991) define denial as "any consciously or unconsciously motivated omission, concealment, or misrepresenta-tion of behaviour or internal experience" (p. 648). Following Gaspar, Palma-Oliveira, and Corral-Verdugo (2010), identifying the degree of environmental awareness provides a means of determining the role of obstacles in environmental inaction. The authors make a distinction between conscious obstacles, which are intentional and controllable, and unconscious obstacles, which unwittingly influence a person's choice. This distinction is also useful for describing how individuals deal with the question of the environment at an individual level.

8.2.2.2 Pathway #1

This decision pathway refers to what we might call pure denial. In this case, denial ensures that the reality of environmental facts remains beyond individual awareness. The discontinuous line indicates that there is no causal relationship, implying that denial intentionally produces inaction in the sense that the individual might act with the aim of deliberately harming the environment (see the chapter on counter-productive behaviors). On the one hand, it seems easier to argue that individuals do not know that they are acting in an environmentally friendly way—or at least, to put it differently, that they are not aware of their inaction. In this case, environmental inaction operates through unconscious obstacles (Gaspar et al. (2010). How should we interpret this situation? The mechanism of repression described by Freud provides some clues. The situation can be illustrated by drawing on the results of a number of studies that have reported how individuals come to favor environmental inaction despite the fact that everything in their immediate environment facilitates the circulation of information. Of course, the methodological foundations on which these studies are based have nothing in common with the method of psychoanalysis. The method of access to the empirical material used is also very different. Freud describes repression as a method of treatment for an impulse. In this respect, repression plays an important role in the Freudian psychological economy. In a sense, an impulse is to the field of psychology what excitement is to the field of physiology. An impulse is a tensing process involving the activation of a need to be satisfied. The outcome of an impulse is the sensation of pleasure. Repression is involved when, rather than providing pleasure, an impulse causes displeasure. The anxiety generated by displeasure is relegated to an unconscious realm by repression and is kept at a distance from the conscious realm. Repression thus involves subtracting from consciousness any sensuous experience that might contribute to causing displeasure rather than pleasure.

Maiteny (2002) reports that the anxiety caused by the societal effects of climate change can cause individuals to seek refuge in the satisfaction afforded by compulsive consumption. Focusing on consumption, Maiteny (2002) showed how people manage the anxiety created by the conflict between their awareness of the increasing social problems raised by the environmental question and their consumption habits when these are perceived as being in conflict with environmental matters. The data indicate that individual accommodation to anxiety is expressed in three different ways: avoidance, adaptation and transformation (the two latter forms of accommodation are discussed below). Through avoidance, individuals seek to divert the effects of anxiety by activating an unconscious process of denial accompanied by an attempt to satisfy their consumption needs through impulse buying behavior. Here, denial replaces anxiety by neutralizing the most disruptive effects on the individual. It is important to acknowledge, however, that a consumption situation differs significantly from a work situation, even though it may be possible to identify several attitudinal and behavioral invariants. Nevertheless, the results of Maiteny (2002) are interesting insofar as they provide a heuristic basis for identifying the different possible responses to anxiety arising from the social issues raised by climate change.

Doherty and Clayton (2011) concluded that environmental anxiety is a form of emotional response arising in relation to a range of threats that individuals perceive as being either real, hypothetical, or fantasized. Through its structures, an organization can perform a neutralizing role by appeasing individual anxiety. This point can be illustrated by a study carried out by Enriquez (1992), who used a Freudian psychoanalytic approach to show that organizational structures serve to channel individual anxiety. Drawing on the results of several field studies, Enriquez set out to show that the structure of social life in an organizational context is shaped by impulses embodied by and in several unconscious authorities (i.e., individual, instinctual, institutional, mythical, group, organizational, and socio-historical authorities). For reasons of space, a detailed overview of the conclusions of Enriquez's study is not possible here, but the key point is that each of these authorities contributes to the channeling of individual anxiety.

Based on the results set out above, we may argue that it is possible for the feeling of environmental anxiety to be channeled by organizations. I propose to explore this idea further. It is now widely acknowledged that, compared to households, organizations play a hugely significant role in environmental degradation, primarily because of the hugely energy-intensive practices required by their administrative, commercial, and industrial activities. The studies discussed in previous chapters showed that individuals can sometimes struggle to transfer their environmental habits from the private sphere to the professional sphere. A solution to this dilemma arises when people with high environmental awareness work for an organization that places the protection of the environment at the heart of its vision. It seems unrealistic to expect organizations to subordinate their activities to the environmental imperative by seeking to achieve a zero-carbon footprint. This raises the question of the regulation of environmental anxiety within organizations where the protection of the environment is not a priority. Here, a sort of compromise emerges between the organization and its members. Through its structures, the organization provides the tools of neutralization that serve to liberate its members from the anxiety inflicted on them by the torments of climate change. However, individuals can find themselves caught in an internal conflict involving a tension between the reassurance provided by the management of their anxiety by organizational structures and the fact that, by virtue of the nature of its commercial and industrial activities, their organization inevitably impacts the environment. In this kind of situation, it may be hypothesized that repression acts as the means by which individuals are able to reconcile the irreconcilable—in other words, to relieve themselves of the burdensome weight of the environmental anxiety associated with the effects of climate change while accepting to ignore the environmental constraints that their work activities impose on the environment.

8.2.2.3   Pathway #2

Pathway #2 involves a justification stage between denial and inaction in the decision-making process. This enables individuals to rationalize their environmental inaction in order to achieve some degree of coherence and consistency. The process of rationalization involves individual strategies aimed at avoiding the burden of discomfort associated with the reality of environmental facts brought to the attention of individuals. This contention is, on the one hand, consistent with the arguments put forward by Gifford (2011), who emphasized that ignorance of climate problems is compatible with a perception of their concrete realities, and, on the other hand, with those of Doherty and Clayton (2011) when emphasizing psychological defenses alongside the principle of social justification to explain how climate change denial makes a lack of concrete response possible.

Lorenzoni et al. (2007) highlighted several individual denial strategies that enable individuals to justify the reasons for their environmental inaction. These strategies operate as neutralization techniques aimed at concealing or obscuring any sense of personal responsibility when individuals catch themselves in the act of being apathetic despite the climate emergency. The various strategies that express denial in a significant way are listed below.

- **Emphasis on the inaction of authorities and industries.** According to the survey conducted by Lorenzoni et al. (2007), nearly 7 out of 10 respondents believe that it is up to governments to take the necessary measures to tackle the issues surrounding the fight against climate change. More than 8 in 10 respondents even believe that, as the chief culprits, industries should take responsibility for the fight against climate change. According to the survey, what this implies is that, at the individual level, inaction is justified by the shouldering of responsibility by political regulatory bodies or by the remedial actions of the main emitters of environmental pollution.
- **Relying on technology.** As a sign of the times, the environment is a topic of choice in science fiction. What movies such as *Soylent Green*, *Interstellar* and *Geostorm* have in common is that they all depict different aspects of the salutary role of technology in helping mankind to cope with an ecological disaster. Relying on technology simply means discharging oneself from any personal responsibility by transferring the burden of finding a solution to a crisis to scientific advances and the resulting technological applications.
- **Skepticism, fatalism, and distrust of information sources.** Faith in science and technology lies in sharp contrast to skepticism. Skepticism and its corollary, distrust of information sources, translates into doubts being expressed about the findings of official reports. Lorenzoni et al. (2007) reported that nearly one in two respondents held the view that the media tend to exaggerate climate change issues.
- **Invoking lack of time.** Time as an obstacle is among the reasons most commonly cited by individuals to justify their inaction. In the case at hand, a question that arises is what people actually mean when they claim to lack time.

Each of these individual strategies is used to justify environmental inaction in different ways, acting as barriers insofar as they are clearly viewed as the reasons why respondents make no effort to reduce their environmental impact.

8.2.3 Stage 3. Beyond Ignorance

8.2.3.1 Awareness and Its Consequences

While ignorance promotes denial, Gifford (2011) argued that it does not condemn individuals to perpetual blindness. According to Gifford, awareness can replace ignorance and cause an individual to take a different path involving responsibilization. However, what remains to be understood is how this substitution process occurs. Stage 3 proposes to give a plausible explanation for how consciousness arises among people with little or no awareness of environmental matters.

Ritter, Borchardt, Vaccaro, Pereira, and Almeida (2015) defined environmental consciousness as "the ability to reshape habits to minimize environmental effects and is affected by cognitive, attitudinal and behaviour components" (p. 509). Based on this definition, depending on whether individuals agree or refuse to significantly alter their way of life, the emergence of consciousness can lead to two different responses. I propose to refer to these responses as inertia and drive. My contention is that a response based on inertia does not lead to a significant change in the way of life, while drive facilitates a reconfiguration of life choices leading to a genuine growth in awareness.

Inertia can be illustrated by a study conducted by Salmela and Varho (2006) on the motivations underlying the use of green electricity (defined by the authors as electricity generated from renewable energy), the results of which highlight an interesting paradox. The authors surveyed a sample of highly educated individuals, pointing implicitly to a high ability to access knowledge, and with a significantly greater interest in environmental matters than their reference group. The respondents indicated that a lack of environmental awareness is often identified as an important barrier in the decision to use green electricity. Salmela and Varho (2006) found no evidence of a strict causal relationship between environmental awareness and consumption behavior. What this finding shows is that a state of environmental awareness is not necessarily reflected by corresponding actions. The personal costs borne as a result of changing consumption modes, the complexity of understanding required on account of the abstract nature of the concept of renewable energy, and institutional policies all act as obstacles that serve to promote inaction. Despite the relatively high degree of environmental awareness observed among the sample surveyed, the authors reported that the participants did not always opt for green electricity. This suggests, on the one hand,

that being aware may not be sufficient by itself to trigger the drive necessary for a significant change in habits and routines (which represents the
main difference with decision pathways #3, 4a, 4b and 5, which involve a
willingness or desire to take concrete action in response to a new awareness). In other words, being aware of a range of environmental issues at
a global level does not necessarily result in individuals acting accordingly
in their everyday life. What may seem to be a paradox at first glance can
be satisfactorily explained when we look at the individual denial strategies
used by individuals to overcome their contradictions.

Drive may stem from the experiential shocks that cause individuals to
reassess their assumptions and beliefs and to alter their environmental
habits (Maiteny, 2002). Lee and Mitchell (1994) noted that "the social
and cognitive context that surrounds the experienced shock provides a
frame of reference within which employees interpret the shock (i.e. a
decision frame)" and "is part of an ongoing context, and the examination of this context helps an employee to interpret the shock along
some key dimensions (e.g. novelty, favorability, threat, or anticipation)"
(p. 61). Many events can cause an experiential shock capable of altering
people's attitudes toward the issue of climate change. Recurrent wildfires,
heatwaves, hurricanes, and intense cold waves (to name but a few) are
increasingly seen as clear evidence of global warming. These events are
anything but new, forming part of the dynamics of our planet. However,
according to many experts, what does appear to be a recent phenomenon
is that these events have increased in intensity. For example, a recent
report by the European Commission found that wildfires are associated with the significant average temperature increase observed across
the regions affected by wildfires (San Miguel-Ayanz et al., 2019). Events
such as these are having a direct impact on the lives of an ever increasing
number of people. They are also tending to encourage growing support
for the environmental cause among citizens. Events such as the global
climate strikes of September 27, 2019 have become a key vehicle for
issuing warnings, or at least for attempting to encourage a new awareness of ecology and environmental matters. It is also interesting to note
that businesses accustomed to managing risks are now starting to become
concerned about the impacts that such events have on their commercial and financial activities. These developments can be illustrated by
the following quote from a report by the International Association of
Insurance Supervisors, which includes the following comment: "It is
difficult to reliably assess the return period for certain extreme weather

events. Insurers may consider that such event risks could only emerge over the long term, allowing for optionality to mitigate through repricing or transfer risk through financial channels (including reinsurance). More evidence/investigation is required to explore the potential for more extreme weather scenarios over short-term timeframes" (p. 40). In my view, it seems reasonable to argue that economic operators combined with the recurring calls for citizen action can contribute to the transition from ignorance to a newfound awareness of the environmental cause.

Personal attitudes toward the environment can act as an obstacle when, in seeking to justify their inaction, individuals emphasize arguments such as temporal or spatial distance. In a study devoted to individual climate change denial strategies, Lorenzoni et al. (2007) reported that 16.3% of the individuals surveyed believed that climate change will affect people in the Third World, 15.6% believed that it will affect the poor, and 7.4% believed that it will mainly impact people living in coastal areas. However, it may be hypothesized that distances diminish with concrete experience, making the climate threat a highly plausible reality and causing previously ignorant individuals to reconsider environmental matters and to take such matters more seriously. Spatial and affective proximity may thus be said to facilitate changes in habits often identified as an obstacle to pro-environmental action (Lorenzoni et al., 2007).

Though necessary, awareness does not appear to be sufficient in itself to trigger individual action. Several variables appear to act as facilitators in this regard. Adopting a macroeconomic approach, Duroy (2005) set out to examine a range of economic and social variables with a view to identifying those with the greatest influence on environmental awareness. Duroy concluded that environmental awareness is most sensitive to psychological and social characteristics defined in terms of subjective wellbeing and the desire to reconnect with nature and appears to be less explained by economic characteristics such as the level of per capita income. However, the results of Duroy's study contrast sharply with other studies indicating that economic costs are often seen as an obstacle that significantly explains environmental inaction (Carrico & Rimer, 2011).

Let us return briefly to the study by Maiteny (2002) on modes of accommodation to environmental anxiety. The mode of accommodation based on denial enables people to free themselves of the tensions generated by irresponsible consumption habits in a context of environmental concern. Maiteny identified two other forms of accommodation. The first involves a logic of adaptation, while the second is based on a logic of transformation. Adaptation is the process by which people aim to reduce their anxiety through a change in purchasing criteria by introducing the principle of ethically and morally responsible choices without substantially changing their consumption habits. Transformation is the process by which people respond to societal issues not only by drastically changing their consumption habits but also by profoundly altering different aspects of their way of life. What Maiteny's findings suggest is that, ultimately, people are able to find within them the necessary psychological and motivational resources to enable them to respond to social injunctions by moving from inertia to action.

8.2.3.2   Behavioral Intention

At this stage, I propose to introduce the notion of the mechanism of behavioral intention combined with the degree of required intensity by way of offering a plausible explanation for understanding how growing environmental awareness leads a person to adopt environmental behaviors. However, as noted in previous chapters, individuals may engage in anti-environmental behaviors more as a result of clumsiness or a lack of awareness than because of a deliberate intention to cause harm. In other words, an appropriate action is defined as the expression of an environmental behavior, while an inappropriate action is defined as the expression of a non-environmental (or anti-environmental) behavior.

Behavioral intention is generally assumed to be the best predictor of behavior. This is because intention carries within it the seeds of action. High intention increases the likelihood that a behavior will be performed, while low intention significantly reduces the likelihood of performance. Studies that have used the theory of planned behavior as a theoretical framework has shown that the predictive capacity of intention for behavior is affected by the degree to which individuals feel that they control the physical and social characteristics of the context in which the behavior is performed. In other words, an intention to behave in an environmentally friendly way does not guarantee that an individual will adopt the associated pro-environmental behavior. The context generates a range of obstacles that hamper individuals' ability to translate their intention into behavior (Plank, 2011). Depending on their nature, obstacles may act as barriers or as constraints.

8.2.3.3   The Reasons for (In)appropriate Environmental Action

As set out in the integrative model, an environmental action can be either appropriate or inappropriate. Decision pathways #3 and #4a apply to individuals who engage in inappropriate environmental actions, while decision pathways #4b and #5 relate to individuals who engage in appropriate environmental actions.

In Chapter 9, I will show that, depending on the nature of job tasks and their type, pro-environmental behaviors depend on employees' degree of decision latitude. However, pro-environmental behaviors also presuppose combining decision with the degree of intensity required. Ciocirlan (2017) noted that engagement in high-intensity environmental behaviors generates high short-term individual costs that may nonetheless be beneficial for the organization in the long run. However, in the case of low-intensity environmental behaviors, Ciocirlan remained relatively vague about both the costs borne by the individual in the short term and the long-term benefits that the organization can expect to reap. By extension, it seems reasonable to assume, however, that low-intensity behaviors generate low short-term individual costs, with, nonetheless, tangible long-term organizational effects. Before going any further, it is important to consider further what the principle of the costs potentially borne by the individual implies and to reiterate what the principle of beneficial effects for the organization might suggest.

The individual cost of required intensity can be assessed in two ways. First, the required intensity is closely related to the principle of inclusion of the behavior in job tasks. For example, Ciocirlan (2017) noted that recycling is a low-intensity activity when it is not a task included in the workload (extra-role) but is defined as a high-intensity activity when it is included in the workload (in-role). Consistent with the management literature, this is explained by the sanctions to which employees may be exposed when they fail to correctly fulfil the job tasks implied by their role and position, unlike tasks performed beyond those which are prescribed, for which no sanction can reasonably be imposed. As noted previously in discussing the results of the study by Chen, Chen, Huang, Long, and Li (2017) on behavioral persistence, the individual cost can also be explained by the risk of generating negative effects on social relationships with peers in a work setting. Lastly, the individual cost can be explained by the potential moral sanctions resulting from social control (see Ohtomo & Hirose, 2007).

An organization may reap benefits from an environmental performance point of view when members behave in environmentally responsible ways (see Chapter 9). For example, an employee's contribution to environmental performance is effective when he or she chooses to attend a meeting remotely via videoconference rather than by travelling to the office (Ones & Dilchert, 2012) or whenever he or she makes a practical contribution to the improvement of environmental practices (Boiral & Paillé, 2012), when he or she contributes to reducing pollution loads or to improving energy efficiency (Di Norcia, 1996), or when he or she communicates, disseminates and shares his or her point of view and ideas on environmental matters (Temminck, Mearns, & Fruhen, 2015).

8.2.3.4   Pathway #3

Decision pathway #3 involves situations in which individuals are driven to act in an environmentally responsible way when they engage in behaviors that involve a high degree of intensity and face obstacles which, depending on the circumstances, operate either as constraints or as barriers. Echoing Chapter 3, inappropriate environmental behavior is viewed more as a matter of behavioral clumsiness that develops over time as a routine rather than the result of a specific intention to act in ways that are deliberately harmful to the environment.

Pathway #3 will be illustrated using the results of Laudenslager, Holt, and Lofgren (2004) and Greaves, Zibarras, and Stride (2013). Both studies are of interest here since they examine several environmental behaviors among the same group of respondents. They are particularly enlightening in that they help to formalize the degree of constraint imposed by the organizational context. If the context does not vary, and if the respondents are the same, the implication is that we need to examine the role of another variable, and that variable is required intensity. The intensity required to behave in an environmentally responsible way at work provides a key for understanding the adoption of appropriate or inappropriate behaviors.

Laudenslager et al. (2004) tested the relevance of the theory of planned behavior in seeking to provide answers to (unsuccessful) attempts by the US Department of Defense to encourage its employees to follow environmental protection programs, the chief aim of which was to improve staff recycling practices across the agency. To this end, the authors examined recycling, but also energy conservation and carpooling practices. Their study provides two findings of interest. The first relates to the level of behavioral intention, which is significantly higher in the case of recycling and energy conservation than it is for carpooling. The second finding relates to the fact that the respondents reported having greater decision latitude over carpooling (by virtue of their significantly higher degree of perceived control) than over recycling and energy conservation practices, while normative pressures to recycle and conserve energy were perceived as being stronger when compared to carpooling. Though requiring low intensity and high decision latitude, the practice of carpooling appears to have acted as a barrier on employees.

Greaves et al. (2013) examined intention to switch off personal computers whenever leaving the desk, intention to use videoconferencing in place of travel, and intention to recycle waste at work. Because the authors limited their study to intention, it is not possible, based on their results, to predict whether the three environmental behaviors studied were indeed affected by contextual characteristics. However, it seems reasonable to argue that, in the case of recycling, lack of recycling facilities and lack of time both acted as obstacles. However, lack of recycling facilities is not the same as lack of time. Lack of facilities acts as a barrier, while a lack of facilities prevents employees from realizing their intention to recycle. On the other hand, lack of time appears to be a constraint that predisposes employees to adopt inappropriate behaviors because of their inability to act in accordance with their intentions. In the case of videoconferencing, the booking process, the number of facilities and the difficulty of using equipment appears to have acted as barriers rather than as constraints. Finally, in the case of energy conservation (switch off PC), leave on for others, risk of forgetting something and short time taken to switch on were found to act less as barriers and more as constraints.

8.2.3.5   *Pathways #4a and #4b*

Pathways #4a and 4b involve pro-environmental behaviors requiring high-intensity engagement on the part of employees. Pathway #4a is a variant of Pathway #3. The difference lies in the fact that the required intensity, though perceived as high, generates neither a constraint nor a barrier. Employees are able to perform appropriate environmental behaviors in their workplace when overcoming constraints (Pathway #4a). However, even if a workplace is equipped with systems and procedures designed to favor greening, more demanding habits may paradoxically be necessary, such that individuals may perceive constraints (Pathway #4b).

For example, studies have demonstrated the role of the physical distance between the physical location of the workstation and a waste facility. Price and Pitt (2012) reported that "frequent recyclers are highly influenced by the "proximity of the facilities" while non-recyclers are influenced by the "distance of facilities" (p. 627). The distance to be traveled appears to be less important than the intention to perform the act itself. In this case, distance is not perceived as a constraint. Employees therefore engage in appropriate environmental actions—i.e., recycling correctly. In the case of employees who are little inclined to recycle, the physical distance to be covered in order to perform the action is used by employees to rationalize their lack of environmental engagement. Based on the findings of this study, it seems reasonable to argue that, for recyclers, intention leads to action because the intensity required by the action is not disrupted by physical distance, while for non-recyclers the distance to be covered requires high intensity, the effect of which is to require a transition from intention to action.

8.2.3.6   Pathway #5

Pathway #5 involves pro-environmental behaviors that require employees to combine both high decision latitude and low-intensity engagement. For the most part, this concerns behaviors that can be performed relatively discretely without the use of any particular system or technology. Behaviors in this category include direct environmental behaviors such as reduction (double-sided printing), reuse (rough paper), repairs of basic work tools and devices, and energy conservation.

Some concluding remarks

In this chapter, an original model was proposed with the aim of describing the decision-making basis for environmental inaction and (in)appropriate environmental action. The integrative model developed here is based on five structuring elements forming the main architecture of the model. Based on these key elements, six individual decision pathways were discussed with a view to providing an account of the various social and cognitive processes that explain employees' predisposition to behave responsibly (or otherwise) toward the environment in a workplace setting.

References

Amel, E. L., Manning, C. M., & Scott, B. A. (2009). Mindfulness and sustainable behavior: Pondering attention and awareness as means for increasing green behavior. *Ecopsychology, 1*(1), 14–25.

Blake, J. (1999). Overcoming the 'value-action gap' in environmental policy: Tensions between national policy and local experience. *Local Environment, 4*(3), 257–278.

Boiral, O., & Paillé, P. (2012). Organizational citizenship behaviour for the environment: Measurement and validation. *Journal of Business Ethics, 109*(4), 431–445.

Carrico, A. R., & Riemer, M. (2011). Motivating energy conservation in the workplace: An evaluation of the use of group-level feedback and peer education. *Journal of Environmental Psychology, 31*(1), 1–13.

Chen, H., Chen, F., Huang, X., Long, R., & Li, W. (2017). Are individuals' environmental behavior always consistent?—An analysis based on spatial difference. *Resources, Conservation and Recycling, 125*, 25–36.

Ciocirlan, C. E. (2017). Environmental workplace behaviors: Definition matters. *Organization & Environment, 30*(1), 51–70.

Di Norcia, V. (1996). Environmental and social performance. *Journal of Business Ethics, 15*(7), 773–784.

Doherty, T. J., & Clayton, S. (2011). The psychological impacts of global climate change. *American Psychologist, 66*(4), 265.

Duroy, Q. M. (2005). *The determinants of environmental awareness and behavior* (Rensselaer Working Papers in Economics 0501).

Enriquez, E. (1992). *L'organisation en analyse.* Paris: PUF.

Gaspar, R. (2013). Understanding the reasons for behavioral failure: A process view of psychosocial barriers and constraints to pro-ecological behavior. *Sustainability, 5*(7), 2960–2975.

Gaspar, R., Palma-Oliveira, J. M., & Corral-Verdugo, V. (2010). Why do people fail to act? Situational barriers and constraints on ecological behavior. In *Psychological approaches to sustainability: Current trends in research, theory and practice* (pp. 269–294). New York: Nova Science Publishers.

Gifford, R. (2011). The dragons of inaction: Psychological barriers that limit climate change mitigation and adaptation. *American Psychologist, 66*, 290–302.

Greaves, M., Zibarras, L. D., & Stride, C. (2013). Using the theory of planned behavior to explore environmental behavioral intentions in the workplace. *Journal of Environmental Psychology, 34*, 109–120.

Issues Paper on Climate Change Risks to the Insurance Sector. The International Association of Insurance Supervisors. (2018, July).

Laudenslager, M. S., Holt, D. T., & Lofgren, S. T. (2004). Understanding air force members' intentions to participate in pro-environmental behaviors: An application of the theory of planned behavior. *Perceptual and Motor Skills,* *98*(3), 1162–1170.

Lee, T. W., & Mitchell, T. R. (1994). An alternative approach: The unfolding model of voluntary employee turnover. *Academy of Management Review,* *19*(1), 51–89.

Li, Y., Johnson, E. J., & Zaval, L. (2011). Local warming: Daily temperature change influences belief in global warming. *Psychological Science, 22,* 454–459.

Lorenzoni, I., Nicholson-Cole, S., & Whitmarsh, L. (2007). Barriers perceived to engaging with climate change among the UK public and their policy implications. *Global Environmental Change, 17*(3–4), 445–459.

Maiteny, P. T. (2002). Mind in the gap: Summary of research exploring "inner" influences on pro-sustainability learning and behavior. *Environmental Education Research, 8,* 299–306.

Molm, L. D., Takahashi, N., & Peterson, G. (2000). Risk and trust in social exchange: An experimental test of a classical proposition. *American Journal of Sociology, 105*(5), 1396–1427.

Ohtomo, S., & Hirose, Y. (2007). The dual-process of reactive and intentional decision-making involved in eco-friendly behavior. *Journal of Environmental Psychology, 27*(2), 117–125.

Ones, D. S., & Dilchert, S. (2012). Employee green behaviors. In S. E. Jackson, D. S. Ones, & S. Dilchert (Eds.), *Managing human resources for environmental sustainability* (Vol. 32). Wiley.

Plank, R. (2011). Green behaviour: Barriers, facilitators and the role of attributions. In *Going green: The psychology of sustainability in the workplace* (pp. 47–58). Leicester: The British Psychological Society.

Price, S., & Pitt, M. (2012). The influence of facilities and environmental values on recycling in an office environment. *Indoor and Built Environment, 21*(5), 622–632.

Ritter, Á. M., Borchardt, M., Vaccaro, G. L., Pereira, G. M., & Almeida, F. (2015). Motivations for promoting the consumption of green products in an emerging country: Exploring attitudes of Brazilian consumers. *Journal of Cleaner Production, 106,* 507–520.

Salmela, S., & Varho, V. (2006). Consumers in the green electricity market in Finland. *Energy Policy, 34*(18), 3669–3683.

San Miguel-Ayanz, J., et al. (2019). *Forest Fires in Europe, Middle East and North Africa 2018* (EUR 29856 EN). Luxembourg: Publications Office of the European Union. https://doi.org/10.2760/1128.

Tanner, C. (1999). Constraints on environmental behaviour. *Journal of Environmental Psychology, 19*(2), 145–157.

Temminck, E., Mearns, K., & Fruhen, L. (2015). Motivating employees towards sustainable behaviour. *Business Strategy and the Environment, 24*(6), 402–412.

Van de Poel, I. (2011). Nuclear energy as a social experiment. *Ethics, Policy & Environment, 14*(3), 285–290.

Vitousek, K. B., Daly, J., & Heiser, C. (1991). Reconstructing the internal world of the eating-disordered individual: Overcoming denial and distortion in self-report. *International Journal of Eating Disorders, 10*(6), 647–666.

Zaval, L., Keenan, E. A., Johnson, E. J., & Weber, E. U. (2014). How warm days increase belief in global warming. *Nature Climate Change, 4*(2), 143.

CHAPTER 9

Greening the Workplace Through Practices and Behavioral Intervention

Abstract This chapter reviews the current state of knowledge on the choices made by and within organizations to encourage, support, and help staff to incorporate environmental considerations into their daily work routines. The chapter sets out to examine our understanding of the measures implemented to reduce the environmental footprint of organizations. It also assesses the effectiveness of such measures from the perspective of environmental performance indicators.

Keywords Environmental performance · Individual latitude · Practices

9.1 Greening the Workplace: From Decisions to Performance

9.1.1 The Limits of Individual Action

In a work context, a person's contribution to environmental performance can be expressed in the form of a wide range of pro-environmental behaviors. Of course, a person's contribution depends on a range of characteristics associated with the type of job performed. Driving a bus, serving a customer, carrying out research to prepare a class, managing a customer account, providing care, delivering an order, and working as an operator on an assembly line are all examples of activities associated with very different jobs. However, what these activities have in common is that they are all structured around a set of tasks that invariably have an impact on the natural environment. Whether it is more or less direct, more or less intense, or more or less conscious, the environmental impact is very real. In other words, in work settings, zero impact is a chimera, an unachievable goal, simply because it is unrealistic. It is unrealistic because of a whole range of contingency factors that significantly influence the choices made by employees and, consequently, restrict their ability to act. The first factor is the level of decision latitude.

The list of environmental behaviors discussed in this book suggests that, in theory at least, there are many options available to an individual to act in an environmentally friendly way in the workplace. This is only partly true. In Chapter 6, I discussed the close similarity between the pro-environmental behaviors observed in and outside the workplace. I also argued that individuals may act differently toward the environment depending on the context in which they find themselves. Depending on an individual's characteristics, a context will tend to limit or constrain environmental engagement to a greater or lesser extent. Thus, in a private (personal) context, an individual's ability to act relative to the range of possibilities available to them will be potentially greater than in an organizational context. For example, in a private context, a person is free to adopt a course of action or behavior that might involve purchasing eco-responsible products. In fact, an individual's scope for action is best examined by taking into account the role performed by that individual in the workplace—a factor that significantly determines the individual's scope for decision-making, referred to in what follows as decision latitude. To understand an individual's scope for action in the environmental field, we need to consider the individual's degree of decision latitude conferred upon them by the type of job performed. The range of possible actions is closely related to decision latitude. Several factors linked to the context of the job performed act potentially as contingent effects on the range of environmental choices available to an employee. These include the type of role, the nature of the tasks performed, and professional status. Clerical, white-collar, and blue-collar jobs are associated with different levels of decision latitude. Likewise, decision-makers (whether senior managers, middle managers or supervisors), and employees do not have the same degree of decision latitude.

9.1.2 Decision Latitude and Constraints on the Ability of Employees to Act

9.1.2.1 Decision latitude

The concept of decision latitude is generally associated with the literature on work stress. More specifically, decision latitude is one of the dimensions of the demand-control model developed by Karasek during the 1980s and 1990s. Whether high or low, decision latitude determines the ability of an individual to bear the mental load associated with the nature of their tasks. In a context of high mental load, high decision latitude enables an individual to cope with stressful episodes by minimizing the harmful effects on their health, while low decision latitude makes stressful work situations difficult to bear and increases the prevalence of health risks. Overall, what the literature on work stress shows is that, within reason, an individual can adapt to a high mental load provided they are able to maintain significant leeway in how they manage their tasks and to draw on their skills and know-how.

What might decision latitude in terms of eco-friendly choices in a work context look like? Before attempting to answer this question, I propose to start from the idea that decision latitude is "the degree to which the respondent can make decisions at work, express creativity, and use and develop skills" (Gallo, Bogart, Vranceanu, & Walt, 2004, p. 64). This definition provides a useful practical framework for understanding the degree of latitude associated with environmental behaviors and implies an ability to influence. However, it is important to note that decision latitude should be distinguished from environmental leadership. Considered at the individual level, environmental leadership involves encouraging an idea, sharing a skill, or promoting a practice with the aim of encouraging other members of the organization to take an interest in the issues and challenges surrounding the greening of their workplace. The concept of environmental leadership reflects an individual's ability to shape the actions and behaviors of others, while the concept of decision latitude discussed here refers to the ability of an individual to behave pro-environmentally given the contingencies associated with the job performed. Put differently, it corresponds to any environmental behavior that can be performed independently without requiring or presupposing any action or approval by another person.

Starting from this basic idea, and as suggested above, we may assume that, in theory, the higher the position of an employee in organization chart, the higher their decision latitude in terms of their ability to act toward the environment. Conversely, an employee in a subordinate position will tend to have a lower degree of decision latitude. Here, decision latitude concerns the extent of behavioral choice rather than any individual willingness to act in an environmentally friendly way in a work context.

To illustrate how employees may or may not be limited in terms of behavioral choices, Fig. 9.1 shows some examples drawn from the list of statements provided by Francoeur et al. (2019). For example, "replacing old appliances by energy-efficient devices" (high decision latitude; direct environmental behaviors) assumes that an individual has a different degree of latitude in terms of decision-making compared to what "encouraging colleagues to recycle" (low decision latitude; indirect environmental behaviors) implies. In combining decision latitude as defined above with the environmental behaviors listed here, we arrive at a wide range of situations. It is beyond the scope of this chapter to list them all.

Examples. Employees in jobs associated with low decision latitude will, in all likelihood, find it easier to engage in direct environmental behaviors that fall under the "conservation" category or in indirect environmental behaviors falling under the "influencing others" category.

On the face of it, reusing, reducing, recycling, and repurposing/repairing represent direct ecological behaviors that offer

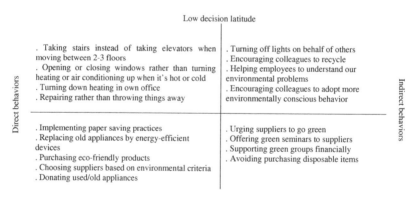

Fig. 9.1 Examples of statements crossing level of latitude and distinction between direct and indirect behaviors

employees the widest range of possibilities for behaving pro-environmentally. Refusing should also be included in the list since refusing to use a specific resource, whether in physical or energy form, may be said to constitute the most pro-environmental of acts—quite simply because refusing is a condition for achieving a zero-carbon footprint. However, because the organization of work activities has attained such a high degree of integration in the use of resources of all kinds, refusal is not a realistic option for many employees.

The greatest latitude concerns the range of actions and behaviors involved in energy conservation. Switching off one's computer or the lights when leaving the office at the end of the day or, by extension, unplugging any device or appliance requiring a supply of electricity stems from an individual and independent decision that does not require another person's approval. Environmental behaviors relating to energy use offer the greatest room for maneuver, though without involving a completely free rein. For example, the use of air conditioning or heating may be impacted according to how the workspace is organized. In the case of an individual premises, low latitude does not influence the ability to open or close windows rather than turning the heating or air conditioning up in warm or cold weather. In the case of a shared premises, low latitude can easily constrain an individual's room for maneuver. In this case, the need to seek approval from colleagues can constrain the degree of individual decision latitude.

Individuals in jobs involving high decision latitude will probably find it easier to engage, in addition to conservation behaviors, in behaviors associated with the "transforming" category. A more nuanced perspective may be needed here. Returning to the example given above of eco-responsible purchasing, something that can be done without difficulty or hindrance in a private context may be possible in an organizational context provided the individual has a sufficient degree of delegation in the decision-making process involved in purchasing eco-responsible products or supplies. However, the range of ecologically responsible alternatives at work is heavily conditioned by the ability of individuals to act freely. Choosing a supplier based on environmental criteria (To, Lam, & Lai 2015) is not the same as choosing an organic meal in the company canteen (Blok, Wesselink, Studynka, & Kemp 2015). Lastly, some findings appear to suggest that decision latitude is not always associated with the role, rank or position held by an employee. As noted below, Cordano and Frieze (2000) reported that three in four environmental managers experienced difficulties in their ability to make the best possible choices to prevent pollution by their organization simply because the choices that seemed most viable to them ran up against the need for approval by decision-making committees.

9.2   Managing Environmental Performance: Connecting Theory to Practice Through Research

9.2.1   Greening the Workplace: A Shared Responsibility

Greening the workplace is above all a matter of shared responsibility. One of its goals is to provide practical solutions in terms of social responsibility to protect future generations from the long-term burden associated with the deterioration of the natural environment caused, in the short term, by the carbon footprint of the industrial, commercial and administrative activities carried out by organizations. This shared responsibility lies at the heart of the conditions required for achieving high environmental performance.

Senior management employees are responsible for defining the environmental vision of an organization (Milliman & Clair, 1996) and for promoting that vision in a top-down way at all levels of the organization. The role of employees down the reporting line is to translate this vision into strategic objectives. Depending on their position along that line, they may be responsible for converting those strategic objectives into operational objectives (Dubois, Astakhova, & Dubois, 2013). The process of conversion applies down to the execution of the most basic tasks. The idea starts from the premise that the vision is clearly defined, that it fits in with the organization's overall mission, that the translation of this vision into strategic and operational objectives is achieved without loss of meaning, that each individual, regardless of their role within the organization, has a perfect understanding of the content of that environmental vision, and, moreover, that each individual is capable of using the resources made available to them in order to act in accordance with that vision. It is only on this condition that the greening of the organization can, in theory, be fully achieved. It seems to me that, in order to be as complete as possible, the measurement of environmental performance should also take into account all these aspects, from the assessment of the vision proposed by top management to what each member of the organization actually does in their day-to-day work in terms of greening by way of realizing that vision.

This also presupposes that individuals at all levels of decision-making have a full and unambiguous understanding of the expectations articulated at higher echelons of the organization, but also of what needs to be done as part of the tasks associated with their job. Having understood the environmental issues and objectives at stake, a requirement such as this also presupposes that each individual incorporates into their work routines the habits that will enable them to act in accordance with the expectations defined at the organizational level. However, individuals may not necessarily have the level of environmental awareness needed to act in accordance with their employer's expectations. Therefore, it is the responsibility of management within organizations to put in place the necessary tools and resources to align the environmental vision with the environmental attitudes expected of employees (Jackson, 2012), to instill an organizational culture centered on the preservation of the environment as a core value (Fernández, Junquera, & Ordiz, 2003), and to promote an environmental culture in the workplace that is conducive to engagement by the greatest possible number of employees (Norton, Parker, Zacher, & Ashkanasy 2015).

9.2.1.1 *Organizational environmental performance*
The idea of shared responsibility for greening the workplace leads on to the question of environmental performance, a matter that also concerns employees at all levels of the organization. Here, a good starting-point is the definition provided by Simpson (2012), according to whom environmental performance may be defined as "a firm's capacity to improve in three main areas: prevention of waste before it occurs, recycling or reducing waste that arises from end-processes, and more efficiently using its material resources" (p. 35). In broad outline, environmental performance refers to objective criteria indicating how an organization seeks to prevent or reduce its environmental impact in terms of ordinary pollution, i.e., the pollution stemming from its routine industrial, commercial and administrative activities and differing from a one-off pollution event occurring as a result of an industrial accident (consider the example of the Lubrizol plant in France in September 2019). Simpson's definition introduces the notion of efficiency, a key term requiring closer examination. An overview of the literature on environmental issues shows that definitions

which make a distinction between levels of environmental performance in terms of effectiveness or efficiency are relatively rare. However, the distinction matters.

Effectiveness and efficiency are not the same, referring, as they do, to related but distinct concepts. Wherein lies the difference between effectiveness and efficiency? An answer to this question can be found in Davis and Pett (2002), who proposed to define efficiency as "the amount of output obtained from a given input" (p. 87) and effectiveness as "the resource-getting ability of an organization" (p. 87), implying a distinction between means and results. If we apply the same idea to the environmental domain, we may say that environmental effectiveness views performance more in terms of the means deployed rather than the results achieved, while environmental efficiency involves viewing performance in terms of the means used in relation to the results achieved. This subtle distinction allows for a better understanding of the concept of environmental performance.

Environmental efficiency is reflected in the use and implementation of environmental practices that help to determine the scale and extent of the means devoted by an organization to preventing its industrial and commercial activities from impacting the environment. We find this idea in various forms and with varying degrees of detail in a number of proposals. For example, Boiral and Henri (2012) proposed the idea of "process and product improvements resulting from the integration of environmental considerations in the operational decisions of the firm" (p. 86), while Husted and de Sousa-Filho (2017) emphasized "the use of good environmental practices, such as implementing pollution control measures, making environmental investments, and setting environmental policies" (p. 94).

In this case, efficiency focuses environmental performance on the question of the environmental consequences arising from the introduction of environmental practices. This approach is reflected, for example, by Blechinger and Shah (2011), who proposed to define environmental performance as "the overall contribution of the policy instrument to direct reduction of GHG-emissions and other indirect environmental impacts such as saved kWhs" (p. 6336). A similar idea can be found in Smeets, Lewandowski, and Faaij (2009), who examined environmental performance in terms of "the greenhouse gas (GHG) emissions, the primary fossil energy use and [...] the impact on fresh water reserves, soil erosion and biodiversity" (p. 1230). The two definitions differ in terms

of intention from definitions that only consider the environmental consequences attributable to organizational activities without really specifying
what is meant by "organizational activities." This position is illustrated,
for example, by Li and Lu (2016), according to whom environmental
performance corresponds to "the outcomes of the firm's environmental
commitments" (p. 463), by Langfield-Smith et al. (2009), who emphasized "the impact of an organisation's activities on the environment,
including the natural systems such as land, air and water as well as on
people and living organisms" (p. 859), and by Burgos-Jiménez, Vázquez-
Brust, Plaza-Úbeda, and Dijkshoorn (2013), who drew attention to "the
actual outcomes of environmental efforts in terms of protecting the
environment" (p. 984).

Ordinary pollution is regulated by implementing environmental practices, including, for example, certifications such as ISO 14000, alongside
a wide range of administrative and industrial procedures. These tools
provide solutions designed to enable organizations to develop environmental performance strategies (Daily & Huang, 2001). However, it is
surprising to find that, behind the range of available definitions, there lies
an often implicit reality largely neglected in research: human intervention. While the introduction of an environmental standard or the use of an
environmental management system may be viewed as necessary conditions
for achieving environmental performance, they are not sufficient in themselves insofar as their introduction and implementation often require daily
corrections and remedies that are only possible through human intervention. For the present purposes, the implication is that environmental
performance cannot really be conceived without taking the human factor
into account. In other words, regardless of whether the study of environmental performance focuses on effectiveness or efficiency, the assumption
is that the starting-point should always involve an approach that places
the question of human intervention at the heart of its analysis.

9.2.1.2   *Environmental performance at the individual level*
It is sometimes argued that environmental performance at the global level
starts with the achievement of environmental performance at the individual level (Ciocirlan, 2017; Gregory-Smith, Wells, Manika, & Graham
2015). More recently, Ones et al. (2018) examined the performative
nature of environmental behaviors in the following terms: Are green
behavior an entirely new dimension of job performance, or do they fit
into one or more broader performance constructs? To fully understand

them, we need to reexamine the foundations underlying the notion of the inclusion of environmental concerns in job tasks discussed in Chapter 3.

In the mid-60s, Katz (1964) examined the theoretical foundations of organizational functioning based on an individual-centered approach. Katz argued that three conditions must be satisfied to enable an organizational system to function effectively. The three conditions set out at the beginning of his paper (p. 132) are: (1) People must be induced to enter and remain within the system; (2) They must carry out their role assignments in a dependable fashion; and (3) There must be innovative and spontaneous activity in achieving organizational objectives which go beyond the specifications of the role. For my purposes, inclusion in job tasks concerns the latter two conditions, which determine what an employer explicitly expects and what they implicitly want from their employee. An organization can legitimately expect its employees to perform the role assigned to them, which broadly involves adhering to various constraints associated with the performance of their work, which is itself assessed in terms of productivity and quality. An organization also expects its staff to engage in other behaviors that not are clearly or explicitly defined. The range of these behaviors is left to the discretion of employees—Katz (1964) speaks of spontaneous innovative behaviors. It is important to note here that Katz presents implicitly desired behaviors as an inherent paradox of any social system. This is because the implication is that management must negotiate between the requirement to comply with instructions and the degree of autonomy granted to employees to enable them to carry out their work.

Examining work behaviors in in-role/extra-role terms helps to further our understanding of the scope of action of employees. At the point beyond which we leave the domain of prescribed tasks that are assumed to be capable of being measured, controlled and assessed to venture into the gray area of real behaviors at work, what people actually do in their work activities has, for several decades, been a research topic that many disciplines in the humanities have sought to understand by using terminologies drawn from different methods or theories. Over time, and following Katz (1964), researchers have found that this gray area provides vital room for maneuver not only for organizations, but also for their members. It is vital for organizations since, very often and without ever really being aware of it, they would not be able to achieve their own performance standards. Indeed, studies have shown that the introduction of environmental standards in an organizational environment presupposes that employees are able to act independently on a day-to-day basis to prevent or correct any instance of poor performance or malfunction (Boiral, 2002).

9.2.1.3 Carbon footprint as an indicator of environmental performance

The study of environmental performance in terms of individual subjectivity requires objective criteria on the basis of which a genuine monitoring tool can be developed to compare the comparable. Any serious analysis of the question of performance in general and of environmental performance in particular must be based on measurable, manipulable and usable criteria fit for assessment purposes. The notion of carbon footprint provides a means of meeting the need for quantification. A good starting-point might be to provide some brief explanations to facilitate understanding of the concept.

Ever since the Kyoto Protocol, the main aim of which was to reduce greenhouse gases, the notion of a ton of carbon dioxide equivalent has become the unit of account generally used to quantify the impact of human activities on the natural environment. CO_2 is a greenhouse gas. Since CO_2 is not the only gas responsible for the greenhouse effect, the term carbon equivalent is also used to refer to the various other gases involved in the greenhouse effect process, such as methane and chlorofluorocarbons (to which the destruction of the ozone layer has been attributed). Without going into a detailed explanation that would be beyond both the scope of this book and my own expertise, and in the spirit of simplicity, suffice to say that CO_2 is generally the carbon molecule considered when studying environmental issues.

A ton of carbon is measured as the level of concentration of CO_2 contained in the atmosphere and corresponds to the ratio of the number of greenhouse gas molecules to the number of air molecules, counted as the number of parts-per-million of particles (source: Actu-Environnement). The level of concentration, measured in parts-per-million (ppm), provides a means of representing as an indicator the changes over time observed in the degree of constraint exerted on the natural environment by the emission of greenhouse gases. A concentration of 400 ppm is defined as a critical threshold. Measured at sea level at a temperature of 25 degrees Celsius, one ton of carbon corresponds to a volume of around 535 cubic meters (source: Figaro.fr, SN Davideau, 05 September 2009).

However, the notion of ton of carbon equivalent may also be thought of as a unit of account. Like any unit of account, it operates as a standardized unit of measurement. In the same way as currencies, it is now used by major industrial and national emitters on trading markets to pursue their potentially harmful activities without fear of retribution. Beyond its economic applications, this standardized unit of account may be viewed as a pedagogical tool that provides a means of translating the effects of human actions into mentally manipulable representations. Standardization enables the notion of ton of carbon equivalent to be used as a helpful point of reference for comparing two things that may be difficult to compare and to estimate the real impact and significance of an individual act.

By way of illustration, one ton of carbon equivalent is equivalent to the amount of energy consumed by three employees over the course of a year in carrying out their work (source: GreenIT.fr). It is estimated that one email generates 19 grams of CO_2, while one online search generates 7 grams (source: Ademe.fr). One ton of carbon equivalent therefore represents 50,000 emails or 142,000 online searches.

Other comparisons have been drawn in research on the choice of mode of transport. According to Bernet (2018), a car "produces 300 kg of CO_2 over the course of a 1000 km return trip. In this case, a car is more polluting than a plane. But people only go on vacation occasionally. With a passenger, emissions are halved, and decrease fourfold when four people travel together. In these cases, driving is far less polluting than flying. However, air travel is at a disadvantage in the case of short trips. Since it uses a significant amount of fuel on takeoff, a plane's carbon footprint is greater over short distances. In the case of Paris, it emits 330 grams per kilometer, but only 189 grams when flying to Beijing." While Bernet compares road and air travel in a vacation context, it seems to me that the same assessment can easily be transferred to a work context. This example provides further evidence of the benefits of carpooling for business travel (for example, when several people from the same firm are required to travel in order to carry out the same assignment).

Another interesting example is provided by Gregory-Smith et al. (2015) in a study devoted to the use of internal social marketing techniques in reducing the use of paper in a work context. The improvement in environmental performance was assessed in terms of CO_2 emissions.

Thus, the reduction in the quantity of printed paper over the course of a year corresponds to an improvement amounting to 690 kilograms of CO_2.

9.2.2 Greening the Workplace Through Practices

9.2.2.1 Resources and costs

The decoupling or dissociation of resource consumption and the associated economic costs is another phenomenon sometimes invoked to explain why people behave differently depending on the environment in which they find themselves. The dissociation has been emphasized in various ways in research on energy consumption (Carrico & Rimmer, 2011; Lo, Peters, & Kok, 2012). One possible explanation is that, in a private setting, energy consumption is a direct domestic cost borne financially by the individual, whereas energy consumption in a workplace setting is a resource made available to the individual to perform a job, the economic cost of which is borne by the organization. The effect of this dissociation may be a form of environmental de-responsibilization among people with little awareness of, or concern for, environmental matters.

When environmental performance is an objective to be pursued, excessive resource consumption can be a legitimate concern when considered at the organizational level. Therefore, it is important for management to provide employees with the means to develop their environmental awareness. To do so, organizations may exploit the potential for individual behavioral plasticity. Here, behavioral plasticity should be understood to mean the way in which an individual's behavior is modified in response to stimuli in their reference environment. Several definitions of the concept have been proposed in a wide range of research fields. In a managerial context, behavioral plasticity is defined by Brockner (1988) as "the extent to which individuals' actions are susceptible to influence by external, and, particularly, social cues" (p. 27). In an organizational environment, though operating at different levels, two types of practices may be used: behavioral intervention practices and green human resource practices.

9.2.2.2 Behavioral change and intervention

Intervention practices designed to effect behavioral change provide organizations with the means of tending toward the greening of workplaces. The foundations of this field of practice are difficult to dissociate from the studies and interventions developed by Lewin and his colleagues in the 1940s and 1950s. Lewin's conceptual principles and practical recommendations were reported in his famous chapter entitled "Group Decision and Social Change" published in 1947 in *Readings in Social Psychology*. The general approach broadly underlying Lewin's thought is rooted in his determination to provide psychology with the epistemological, theoretical and methodological tools to become a scientific discipline on a par with physics (see Chapter 7). As an anecdote, it is worth noting that around the same time a similar movement from the physical to the social sciences was being mapped out. For example, the Italian physicist Ettore Majorana, whose long-forgotten work is now gradually being rediscovered and praised for its scale and modernity, proposed a profound reflection on the possibilities of a "formal analogy between the statistical laws observed in physics and in the social sciences" in a posthumous paper (quotation from Mantagna cited in Bontems, 2013).

The conceptual principles developed by Lewin are based on the simple idea that human behavior is the manifestation of a latent force field. This field is the expression, at a given time, of the relationship between opposing forces. This relationship is described as a state of "quasi-stationary equilibrium." The key point in Lewin's approach is that this equilibrium is the result of an ongoing social process (Lewin, 1947). It can be modified, so Lewis argues, by having an effect on the antagonism of forces. The goal of intervention practices is precisely to modify this antagonism in such a way as to tend toward the desired behavior. A practical intervention can help to reconfigure the conditions of the equilibrium of the force field in order, in theory, to encourage individuals subject to intervention to adopt the behaviors targeted by the experimenter. Lewin sought to demonstrate the validity of his approach through experiments reported in his chapter on food choices and habits and on resistance to change in an industrial context.

Lewin's approach has given rise to an important stream of research for the study of behavioral modifications in an environmental context. For example, Staddon et al. (2016) published a systematic review of interventions designed to change behavior and save energy in the workplace. Their review included 22 studies examined and interpreted using the Behaviour Change Wheel (BCW) research framework imported from health research. BWC examines health behavior changes through nine forms of intervention: education (Increasing knowledge or understanding), persuasion (Using communication to induce positive or negative feelings or stimulate action), incentivization (Creating expectation of reward), coercion (Creating expectation of punishment or cost), training (Imparting skills), restriction (Using rules to reduce the opportunity to engage in the target behavior), environmental restructuring (Changing the physical or social context), modeling (Providing an example for people to aspire to or imitate), and enablement (Increasing means/reducing barriers to increase capability or opportunity). The study by Staddon et al. (2016) has two main benefits for my purposes. The first is that it focuses on pro-environmental behaviors associated with high decision latitude at the individual level. Second, it provides a good illustration of the possible levers for action in terms of greening the workplace, along with empirically-based findings. The main results are as follows:

- Enablement is the form of intervention that offers the greatest potential for encouraging employees to change their behavior and adopt environmental behaviors conducive to energy consumption reduction (e.g., switching off lights, turning off computers). Enablement emphasizes psychological capability, motivations and the opportunities that enable employees to overcome obstacles in the workplace.
- Intervention practices focused on influence and adherence to social norms are considered to be more effective than practices based on modeling, peer education, and social persuasion.
- The effectiveness of these practices is reflected by the energy efficiency gains achieved, which, according to the studies reviewed, range between 4% and 51%.

Overall, the study by Staddon et al. (2016) demonstrates that the findings of studies devoted to the role of intervention practices in modifying environmental behaviors have generally been consistent with the Lewinian tradition. Compared to practices that tend to position individuals in a passive role or mobilize them using constraint, practices that engage employees on a voluntary basis offer the most effective lever for promoting behavioral change.

9.2.2.3 Green Human Resource Management practices

The need to consider environmental matters in an organizational context has led to the need to review the Human Resource Management approach and to question the role of its most common practices. The focus of GHRM practices is also to meet the expectations of stakeholders performing their environmental monitoring activity in relation to the actions of organizations. This need has led to the emergence of a new branch of Human Resources Management that has come to be known as Green Human Resource Management (GHRM).

The study by Renwick, Maguire and Redman (2013) was a major contributing factor in the emergence of this new field—a field increasingly structured in recent years around a community of active researchers. According to Amrutha and Geetha (2020), more than half of the papers devoted to GRHM appeared between 2016 and 2019. However, these recent developments should not obscure the earliest thoughts on the subject reported in the volume edited by Whermeyer (1996) and published under the title *Greening the People*, which offers one of the first substantive considerations of the role of human resources in a context of environmental transformation in an organizational setting. GHRM practices play a key role at each stage of the employee life-cycle from attracting newcomers (Pham & Paillé, 2020) to staff retention (Benn, Teo, & Martin 2015).

Tang et al. (2018) described GHRM practices by drawing on the relevant literature. Only the main propositions are reproduced below:

- *Green recruitment and selection*: "The preference of the organization is to select candidates who are committed and sensitive to environmental issues and willing to contribute through internal or external recruitment";
- *Green training*: "The organization implements a system of learning practices related to environmental issues to improve employees' awareness and their environmental management skills";
- *Green performance management*: Based on "the vision of environmental management, the organization will appraise employees' environmental results in the [entire] operational process to assess their contribution to organizational goals";
- *Green rewards*: "Financial and non-financial rewards for organizational members whose attitude or behavior is conductive to environmental management";
- *Green employee involvement*: "An opportunity is provided for employees to engage in environmental management. The broad types include participation, support culture and tacit knowledge,

which aim to stimulate members' commitment to the environmental management of the organization."

GHRM practices are generally examined using the Ability-Motivation-Opportunity framework (Amrutha and Geetha, 2020). On this subject, Renwick et al. (2013) posited that "HRM works through increasing employees' *Ability* through attracting and developing high-performing employees; enhancing employees' *Motivation* and commitment through practices such as contingent rewards and effective performance management (PM); and providing employees with the *Opportunity* to engage in knowledge-sharing and problem-solving activities via employee involvement (EI) programmes" (p. 2).

Lastly, Zibarras, and Coan (2015) surveyed a sample of 214 individuals, most of whom were managers (16% of the respondents worked in a nonmanagerial position), focusing on how GHRM practices within the organization relate to the pro-environmental behaviors of employees. The findings highlight two key points. First, the prevalence of green rewards, employee empowerment and various environmental performance indicators tends to be greater in large firms (with more than 250 employees) than in small firms (with fewer than 250 employees). Second, management involvement (more than 35% of the responses), employee empowerment (more than 27% of the responses) and training (more than 17% of the responses), and green rewards (8% of the responses) were referred to as the most effective GRHM practices for encouraging employees to behave in an environmentally responsible way in their day-to-day work.

Some Concluding Remarks

In previous chapters, I emphasized the close similarity between the environmental behaviors performed by an individual when engaging with different spheres or domains of activity. I also suggested that this similarity is no guarantee of behavioral continuity because of obstacles that are inherent to organizational contexts. Lastly, drawing on the notion of decision-making autonomy, several reasons were proposed to explain why individuals are limited in the range of environmental behaviors that they can actually perform in practice. An individual's contribution to environmental performance is thereby limited. The implementation of practices aimed at changing individual attitudes and behaviors is a means of moving toward the greening of workplaces.

REFERENCES

Amrutha, V. N., & Geetha, S. N. (2020). A systematic review on green human resource management: Implications for social sustainability. *Journal of Cleaner Production, 247,* 119131.

Benn, S., Teo, S. T., & Martin, A. (2015). Employee participation and engagement in working for the environment. *Personnel Review, 44,* 492–510.

Bernet, C. (2018). https://www.24heures.ch/economie/bilan-carbone/story/23861440.

Blechinger, P. F. H., & Shah, K. U. (2011). A multi-criteria evaluation of policy instruments for climate change mitigation in the power generation sector of Trinidad and Tobago. *Energy Policy, 39*(10), 6331–6343.

Blok, V., Wesselink, R., Studynka, O., & Kemp, R. (2015). Encouraging sustainability in the workplace: A survey on the pro-environmental behaviour of university employees. *Journal of Cleaner Production, 106,* 55–67.

Boiral, O. (2002). Tacit knowledge and environmental management. *Long Range Planning, 35*(3), 291–317.

Boiral, O., & Henri, J. F. (2012). Modelling the impact of ISO 14001 on environmental performance: A comparative approach. *Journal of Environmental Management, 99,* 84–97.

Bontems, V. (2013). L'épistémologie Transversale D'ettore Majorana. *Revue de Synthèse, 134*(1), 29–51.

Brockner, J. (1988). *Self-esteem at work: Research, theory, and practice.* Lexington Books/DC Heath and Com.

Carrico, A. R., & Riemer, M. (2011). Motivating energy conservation in the workplace: An evaluation of the use of group-level feedback and peer education. *Journal of Environmental Psychology, 31*(1), 1–13.

Ciocirlan, C. E. (2017). Environmental workplace behaviors: Definition matters. *Organization & Environment, 30*(1), 51–70.

Cordano, M., & Frieze, I. H. (2000). Pollution reduction preferences of US environmental managers: Applying Ajzen's theory of planned behavior. *Academy of Management Journal, 43*(4), 627–641.

Daily, B. F., & Huang, S. (2001). Achieving sustainability through attention to human resource factors in environmental management. *International Journal of Operations & Production Management, 21*(12), 1539–1552.

Davis, P. S., & Pett, T. L. (2002). Measuring organizational efficiency and effectiveness. *Journal of Management Research, 2*(2), 87–97.

de Burgos-Jiménez, J., Vázquez-Brust, D., Plaza-Úbeda, J. A., & Dijkshoorn, J. (2013). Environmental protection and financial performance: An empirical analysis in Wales. *International Journal of Operations & Production Management, 33*(8), 981–1018.

DuBois, C. L., Astakhova, M. N., & DuBois, D. A. (2013). Motivating behavior change to support organizational environmental sustainability goals. *Green Organizations: Driving Change with IO Psychology*, 186–207.

Fernández, E., Junquera, B., & Ordiz, M. (2003). Organizational culture and human resources in the environmental issue: A review of the literature. *International Journal of Human Resource Management, 14*(4), 634–656.

Francoeur, V., Paillé, P., Yuriev, A., & Boiral, O. (2019). The measurement of green workplace behaviors: A systematic review. *Organization & Environment*. https://doi.org/10.1177/1086026619837125.

Gallo, L. C., Bogart, L. M., Vranceanu, A. M., & Walt, L. C. (2004). Job characteristics, occupational status, and ambulatory cardiovascular activity in women. *Annals of Behavioral Medicine, 28*(1), 62–73.

Gregory-Smith, D., Wells, V. K., Manika, D., & Graham, S. (2015). An environmental social marketing intervention among employees: Assessing attitude and behaviour change. *Journal of Marketing Management, 31*(3–4), 336–377.

Husted, B. W., & de Sousa-Filho, J. M. (2017). The impact of sustainability governance, country stakeholder orientation, and country risk on environmental, social, and governance performance. *Journal of Cleaner Production, 155*, 93–102.

Jackson, S. E. (2012). Building empirical foundations to inform the future practice of environmental sustainability. In S. E. Jackson, D. S. Ones, & S. Dilchert (Eds.), *Managing human resources for environmental sustainability* (pp. 416–432). Wiley.

Katz, D. (1964). The motivational basis of organizational behavior. *Behavioral Science, 9*(2), 131–146.

Langfield-Smith, K., Thorne, H., Hilton, R. (2009). Management accounting: Information for creating and managing value (5th ed.). Sydney, NSW, Australia: McGraw-Hill.

Lewin, K. (1947). Group decision and social change. In T. M. Neweomb and E. L. Hartley (Eds.), *Readings in Social Psychology* (pp. 340–44). Henry Holt and Co.

Li, W., & Lu, X. (2016). Institutional interest, ownership type, and environmental capital expenditures: Evidence from the most polluting Chinese listed firms. *Journal of Business Ethics, 138*(3), 459–476.

Lo, S. H., Peters, G. J. Y., & Kok, G. (2012). Energy-related behaviors in office buildings: A qualitative study on individual and organisational determinants. *Applied Psychology, 61*(2), 227–249.

Milliman, J., & Clair, J. (1996). Best environmental HRM practices in the U.S. In W. Wehrmeyer (Ed.), *Greening people: Human resources and environmental management* (pp. 49–73). Greenleaf.

Norton, T. A., Parker, S. L., Zacher, H., & Ashkanasy, N. M. (2015). Employee green behavior: A theoretical framework, multilevel review, and future research agenda. *Organization & Environment, 28*(1), 103–125.

Ones, D. S., Wiernik, B. M., Dilchert, S., & Klein, R. M. (2018). Multiple domains and categories of employee green behaviours: More than conservation. In *Research handbook on employee pro-environmental behaviour*. Edward Elgar Publishing.

Pham, D. D., & Paillé, P. (2020). Green recruitment and selection: An Insight of Green Pattern. *International Journal of Manpower, 41*(3), 258–272.

Renwick, D. W. S., Redman, T., & Maguire, S. (2013). Green human resource management: A review and research agenda. *International Journal of Management Reviews, 15*(1), 1–14.

Simpson, D. (2012). Knowledge resources as a mediator of the relationship between recycling pressures and environmental performance. *Journal of Cleaner Production, 22*(1), 32–41.

Smeets, E. M., Lewandowski, I. M., & Faaij, A. P. (2009). The economical and environmental performance of miscanthus and switchgrass production and supply chains in a European setting. *Renewable and Sustainable Energy Reviews, 13*(6–7), 1230–1245.

Staddon, S. C., Cycil, C., Goulden, M., Leygue, C., & Spence, A. (2016). Intervening to change behaviour and save energy in the workplace: A systematic review of available evidence. *Energy Research & Social Science, 17,* 30–51.

Tang, G., Chen, Y., Jiang, Y., Paille, P., & Jia, J. (2018). Green human resource management practices: Scale development and validity. *Asia Pacific Journal of Human Resources, 56*(1), 31–55.

To, W. M., Lam, K. H., & Lai, T. M. (2015). Importance-performance ratings for environmental practices among Hong Kong professional-level employees. *Journal of Cleaner Production, 108,* 699–706.

Zibarras, L. D., & Coan, P. (2015). HRM practices used to promote pro-environmental behavior: A UK survey. *The International Journal of Human Resource Management, 26*(16), 2121–2142.

Index

© The Editor(s) (if applicable) and The Author(s), under exclusive licence to Springer Nature Switzerland AG 2020
P. Paillé, *Greening the Workplace*,
https://doi.org/10.1007/978-3-030-58388-0

CPSIA information can be obtained
at www.ICGtesting.com
Printed in the USA
LVHW091940250121
677440LV00004B/79

9 783030 583873